Please God, Let There Be
Another Boom

Also by Grant McDowell . . .

Bruised Knuckles and Other Lessons in Faith

Please God, Let There Be Another Boom

Faith and Hope at Work in Lean Times and Good Times

Grant McDowell

WestBow Press books may be ordered through booksellers or by contacting:

WestBow Press
A Division of Thomas Nelson
1663 Liberty Drive
Bloomington, IN 47403
www.westbowpress.com
1-(866) 928-1240

ISBN: 978-1-4497-2473-3 (sc)

Library of Congress Control Number: 2011961085

Printed in the United States of America

WestBow Press rev. date: 12/16/2011

Contents

Acknowledgements

I am indebted to my loving wife Donna for consenting to repeatedly proof-read my manuscripts. Her insights and questions helped me cull irrelevant material and sharpen what remains. My children, Nathan, David and Holly, have not only postponed family events and celebrations because of my work, but by sharing their experiences in the blue-collar world, they have deepened my resolve to address issues of faith at work.

I am indebted to the feedback of Haddon Robinson and Will Messenger, whose questions and principled teaching have encouraged me. Also, the people of Leduc Alliance Church have patiently answered questions about conditions in their places of work. Their faithfulness to the Lord, in places that are sometimes difficult, inspires me.

The business community of Leduc and area has continually provided a vibrant background for my study of the blue-collar workplace and the issues of life and work in general. And, finally, I thank employers in my blue-collar upbringing who helped shape, for better or worse, my perspective on work.

When you consider that more than 50 percent of a person's waking hours are in the workplace, why not enjoy the experience? If you can find "joy in the job, as well as in the journey," your work can become a place that brings immense satisfaction as you deliver your very best! Insightful and instructional, Grant McDowell's investment of time and research has resulted in a relevant and practical guide for those looking to connect God's purpose and their place of work. Knowing his commitment to those within his community, his genuine interest in mentoring and developing others, thank you Grant for the privilege of previewing your new book.

Jim Ewing, Co-Founder

Pro-Vision Solutions Inc.
Edmonton, Alberta (Canada)
Mentorship BLOG: http://provision-mentorship.blogspot.com/

Noah, Abraham, Isaac, Jacob, Sarah, Joseph, Moses, Joshua, and David are all referred to in Hebrews 11 as people of faith . . . and they all had jobs—construction, agriculture, government, politics and the military. They served God—at work—and they have left an example for how Canadians can serve God—at work. This book speaks of Christians who serve God through their work, in the times of Scripture, and today. May it challenge you to be a Hebrews 11 Christian—at work.

Paul Richardson

Former President of Christian Business Ministries Canada

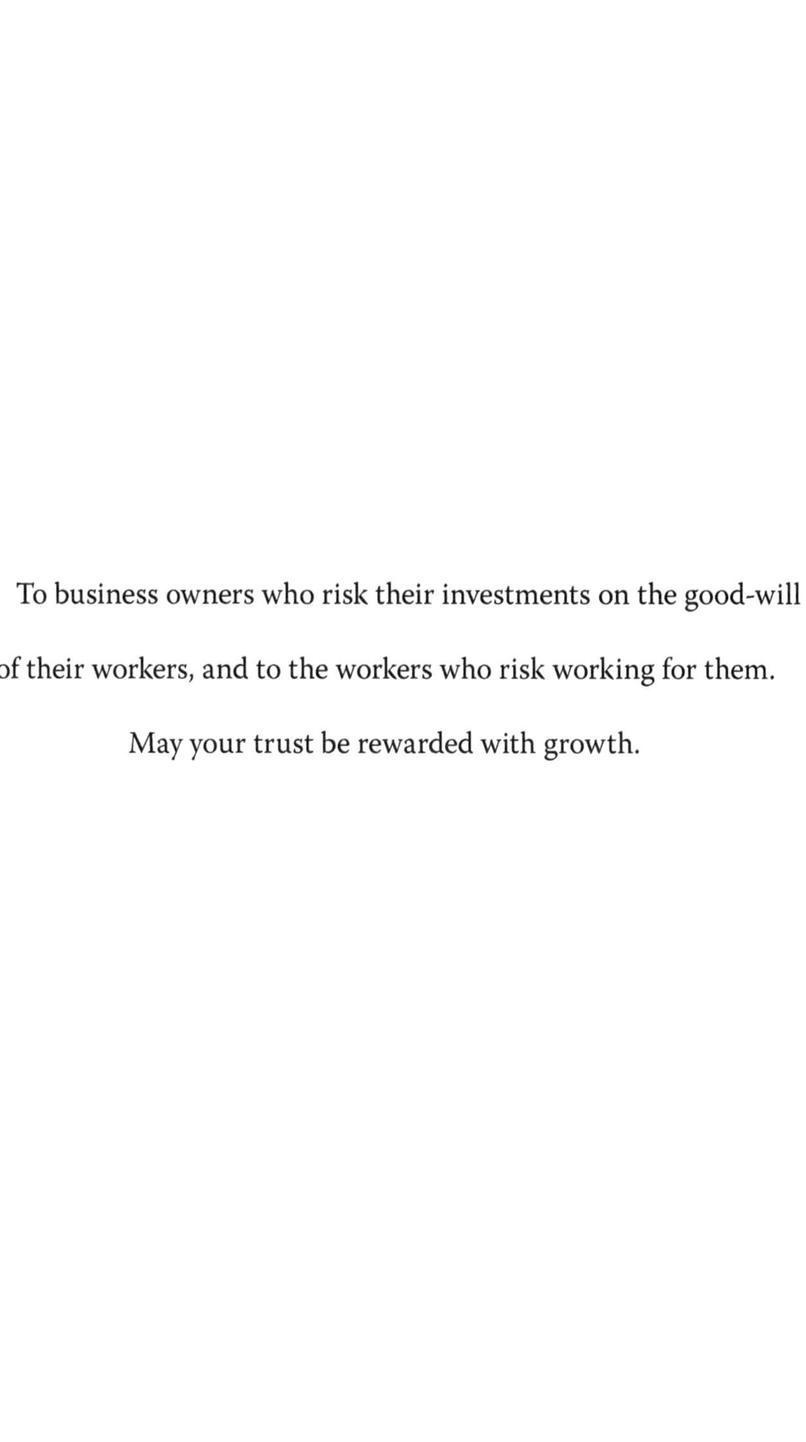

To business owners who risk their investments on the good-will of their workers, and to the workers who risk working for them.

May your trust be rewarded with growth.

Introduction

The Sunday morning adult elective moved along fine until I asked what the group thought of the principal lesson. As though he had rehearsed, the big farmer whose frame dominated the front row blurted out, "Don't wanna think; just tell us the answers." He is not the only one. Christians have not always wanted to think about integrating faith in Christ with day-to-day work. Therefore, the critical question is "How can we help blue-collar workers, regardless of their knowledge of the Bible, integrate faith and work?"

Most attempts to close the faith at work gap target leaders in business while trades and labor are not being given the message that their work praises the Lord. For example, worship services, small group Bible studies, and even board meetings are seen as sacred tasks, but Christians may be unsure whether God is interested in their lives from 9 to 5, or, in some cases, from 6 a.m. or earlier until 6 p.m. or later.

The assumption that God favors the role of career minister more than the blue-collar worker deepens the divide between faith and work. For example, one speaker explained how he came to faith following a terrible industrial accident. During his recovery he sensed God's call to pastoral ministry. His testimony, using the language of calling, explicitly claimed that he had been promoted to a higher purpose than his previous job in the oil industry. Perhaps extreme crises elevate the importance of pastoral work in the minds of people who face such experiences. Moreover, there is a deeply rooted conviction among many Christians that the work God values happens in church buildings, though some admit that God might also value the work of executives in leadership roles. Those of us who pastor churches share some responsibility for creating this divide between faith and work. I have heard frustrated leaders of an organization that ministers to

Christians in business saying, "My pastor doesn't get it!" However, when a mentor asked me what surprised me about engaging in a ministry that aims to integrate faith and work, I said I was surprised at how difficult this work can be. Workers sometimes would rather leave their faith at church or at home than take it to the job.

Sunki Bang suggests business and mission have been viewed in several different ways. Bang's delineation of business is as follows:

- Business and mission—two isolated activities
- Business for mission—using the proceeds of business as a way of financing mission
- Business as a platform for mission—work and professional life as a means of channeling mission throughout the world (in Korea they are called "Businaries")
- Mission in business—hiring non-believers with a view to leading them to Christ, offering chaplaincy services.
- Business as mission—business as part of the mission of God in the world.[1]

Seeing business as ministry, like seeing labor as ministry, leads one to integrate faith and work.

This problem must be addressed because, from the opening chapters of Genesis, Scripture describes work as essential to God's purpose for people. However, blue-collar workers often do not know that their work matters to God. We dare not treat work as an exterior reality Christians must somehow cope with, while treating faith as an interior reality to keep uncontaminated by trades, labor or service work. Work itself is God's ministry rather than just a platform for ministry.

---

1 Sunki Bang, "Tensions in Witness," *Vocatio*, 1, no. 2, July 1998, 17-18, quoted in Paul Stevens, *Doing God's Business* (Grand Rapids: Eerdmans, 2006), 80.

PART ONE

IN THE BEGINNING WORK WAS GOOD

The bright yellow sticker said, in bold, black, irreverent lettering, "Please God, let there be another oil boom and this time I promise I won't ____ it all away." The sticker, in the window of a pickup truck, revealed the frustration and stubborn hope of a workforce whose existence depends on the price of oil. The sticker appeared in the mid 1980s in a small city in the province of Alberta next to a sprawling industrial park, which seemed to have almost as many empty buildings as businesses. As well, some homeowners, owing more to the bank than the market value of their homes, had walked away from their mortgages. Besides illustrating the economy, the crude sticker depicted aspects of blue-collar culture: blue-collar workers prefer blunt, direct talk; they depend on economic forces beyond their control; and they want faith, if they care about it at all, to relate to their everyday circumstances. Though the yellow sticker's "prayer" was irreverent, it betrayed a need for a practical view of God's involvement in the workplace.

A large, interdenominational mission conference illustrated the church's failure to help workers integrate faith with the workplace.[2] Although one set of conference seminars addressed this subject, presenters focused almost entirely on how to verbally share one's faith. In other words, the business community is seen as a new frontier for

---

[2] Conferences on world missions are healthy, credible opportunities to teach and inspire Christ's followers for service. The point criticized here is the assumption that evangelism is the only redeeming activity in the workplace.

missions. As a result, Bible studies and small group materials usually focus on how to evangelize effectively in the workplace. Instead of viewing work *as* mission, many leaders and writers view work as a platform *for* mission. Consequently, small group material seldom addresses the practical issues facing the blue-collar worker; rather it repackages evangelistic technique for the workplace. Although there is a place for verbal witness at work, this book focuses on how we can help workers like the welding shop laborer and the truck driver appreciate God's role in their workplaces. But first, we focus on God as a worker, on his image in workers, and on his mandate that people should work.

CHAPTER 1

The Creator Works

A laborer who works in a welding shop located in an industrial park as big as a medium-sized city might wonder how a holy God regards his work. His pastor believes and teaches that God values work, but the laborer's memory replays the sarcastic, filthy names the lead hand calls him. His workplace culture seems to make work a necessary evil, and so mocks the truth that work is inherently good. Yet, the Bible reveals God himself as a worker: "By the seventh day God had finished the work he had been doing; so on the seventh day he rested from all his work. And God blessed the seventh day and made it holy, because on it he rested from all the work of creating that he had done." (Genesis 2:2,3) God worked in creation. Banks writes

> The biblical writings often depict God as a craftsperson at work, for example, as a potter, metalworker, weaver, knitter, stonemason, carpenter, builder, or architect. In their own ways these occupations, as well as others ranging from gardening and landscape artistry, to interior design and urban planning, can be earthly manifestations of heavenly work. But any occupation or activity that has a touch of originality about it reflects something of God's creative work.[3]

---

[3] Robert Banks, "The Place of Work in the Divine Economy," in *Faith Goes to Work*, ed. Robert Banks (New York: The Alban Institute, 1993), 23.

Genesis shows God's workmanship: the sky (1:7), the sun and moon (1:16), the sea creatures, the birds and the animals (1:20-25). And God created man in his own image on day six of creation (1:27). As Genesis 2:2 says, God worked and then rested. He surveyed all he had made and saw that it was very good. (Genesis 1:31)

Furthermore, the Psalms depict God's work. Psalm 19:1, for example, says, "The heavens declare the glory of God; the skies proclaim the work of his hands." Other Psalms picture God the worker: "When I consider your heavens, the work of your fingers, the moon and the stars, which you have set in place, what is man that you are mindful of him, the son of man that you care for him?" (8:3,4) Psalm 107 appeals to those in dangerous situations to, ". . . give thanks to the LORD for his unfailing love and his wonderful deeds for men . . ." (vv. 8,15,21,31) In this Psalm, we see God actively involved, working in the circumstances of his people, drawing to himself those who have ignored or rejected his love. And Psalm 104:10-22 describes God's active work, sustaining the environment where laborers work.

As he begins sweeping bits of slag, chunks of dried mud, and other garbage, the laborer mulls over the possibility that God might see work as valuable because God himself works. Genesis also expresses God's work through the words "form" (2:7,8,19), "build" (2:22), and "plant" (2:8). Maybe there is a connection between Sunday and Monday after all. The Creator values hands-on involvement with his creation. God is active. Throughout his creation story are the words "make" and "create."[4]

The God of the Bible is distinct from the gods of other religions, which would not subject themselves to a servant role that includes making things for others to enjoy. In the Bible, for example, the Messiah himself was a carpenter who had been born in a stable where humble shepherds visited him. As a result, the laborer can work with awareness that God enters into service work.

While Greek philosophers viewed work as beneath the dignity of their deities, and Greek thinkers viewed people as either noble men of leisure or slaves destined for menial tasks, Christian theology sees

---

4 Foster R. McCurley and John H. Reumann, "Work in the Providence of God," in *Work as Praise*, eds. George W. Forell and William H. Lazareth., (Philadelphia: Fortress Press, 1979), 29, 30.

work with one's hands as noble and godly.[5] Carl Henry illustrates this with the example of God the Son: "It is inconceivable that he would consider his daily task a chore and not a challenge; that he should be content with shoddy and disreputable work instead of showing himself a master craftsman."[6] And G.F. Macleod writes, "God loves the material element He has created and finds it in no way inconsistent with His spiritual dignity to stoop down and to unite Himself with the earth: with flesh and blood . . ."[7]

5 Carl Henry, *Aspects of Christian Social Ethics,* (Grand Rapids: Eerdmans, 1980), 49.

6 Ibid., 52.

7 George F. MacLeod, *Only One Way Left,* (Glasgow: The Iona Community, n.d.), 156.

CHAPTER 2

The Creator's Image at Work

"So God created man in his own image, in the image of God he created him; male and female he created them." (Genesis 1:27) Man and woman were the climax of God's creation, and he designed them to work. "At the same time that human beings share a common origin, each of us contributes a unique way of being and a particular mode of doing as an expression of our being."[8]

Therefore, work is dignified because workers have dignity in God's image; workers give their work dignity; work does not give workers dignity, but it is an expression of their faith in God as their designer. Both women and men are bound to this destiny of work, because God created them to compliment one another (Genesis 2:18,20).[9]

Therefore, work has meaning because, through work, workers display the image of God. And one should note that workers do not give meaning to work by making it into a Christian institution. For example, importing Bible studies into the workplace lunch room is not evidence our view of work has become Christian. Moreover, workers should adopt the value of treating others kindly *at* work, yet must also embrace the sacred nature *of* work itself. In fact, God has given people this destiny of sharing his work and continuing what he

8 Camilla Burns, "The Call of Creation," in *Revisiting the Idea of Vocation*, ed. John C. Haughey, S. J., (Washington: Catholic University of America Press, 2004), 24.

9 Edwin G. Kaiser, *Theology of Work*, (Westminster, Maryland: The Newman Press, 1966), 54.

began at creation.[10] Furthermore, God does not view workers as slaves who must work for him. Instead, God gave a garden to be tilled and preserved for the benefit of the workers who live in it.[11] God values the laborer's work as an expression of his image.

The truck driver plots his route to the address where he will unload tons of construction material. After guiding the huge vehicle through streets designed for small cars, he carefully backs the long load on to the site. With the boom crane he lowers lifts of gypsum to the ground with artful dexterity. Then he and a laborer balance several hundred pounds of board between them and begin carrying the material into the new home. "Is God in this?" he wonders.

Does God really want anything to do with life in the world? Some Christians do not think he does. As one man said, "Before I received the Holy Spirit, I . . . worried all the time about political and economic issues. But now that I'm Spirit-filled, I let others worry about those things. I'm just too busy getting to know Jesus better!"[12]

Richard Mouw relates an experience he had preaching in a church where he was warned the people did not believe Christianity had anything to do with politics. The service opened with the hymn, "O Worship the King." A children's choir sang, "Jesus loves the little children . . . red and yellow, black and white, they are precious in his sight." Mouw reminded the people they had already established that Jesus is King and that all races are precious to the King. Now the question was what they were going to do to address concerns about life on reservations, for example. Mouw says Christians often call Jesus "King" as a figure of speech, but states that when early Christians called Jesus "Lord," they were rejecting all political leaders' claims to supreme lordship.[13]

God is Lord over construction sites and heavy loads as well as political decisions, whether workers or leaders acknowledge him or not. Created in his image, laborers work to create the world they want to live in. They are not silent observers—spectators on the sidelines

---

10 Ibid., 53.

11 Foster R. McCurley and John H. Reumann, "Work in the Providence of God," 30.

12 Richard J. Mouw, *Called to Holy Worldliness,* (Philadelphia: Fortress Press, 1980), 5,7.

13 Ibid. 7,8.

of a world God runs on puppet strings. By God's grace, they work in partnership with his Spirit to make this world more perfect, or at least livable. This God-given dignity motivates them to pray, think and act with a particular end in view. That end is the day when all things will be restored to perfect order under Christ. In the mean time, laborers work in the daily grind of life and unlock new methods and materials. Michael Novak writes,

> The Creator, in Pope John Paul II's vision, has hidden within creation untold riches, resources, and possibilities which it is the vocation of humans to discover and to realize, for the common good of all. He, therefore, places great emphasis upon invention and discovery . . . It is through such discovery that man "subdues the earth."[14]

Similarly, Carl Henry writes, "Created in the spiritual and moral image of God (Gen. 1:26-28), man's larger vocation is to rule the earth in obedience to the Ruler of all things."[15] The blue-collar worker images God at work by bringing order out of chaos.

Paul Stevens, on the other hand, illustrates how many Christians view work. When he left pastoral ministry and took up construction, some said, "You have left the ministry. You are wasting your talents. You are denying your call."[16] But work is a means by which workers demonstrate the image of God. Dorothy Sayers proposes,

> . . . that work is not, primarily, a thing one does to live, but the thing one lives to do. It is, or, it should be, the full expression of the worker's faculties, the thing in which he finds spiritual, mental, and bodily satisfaction, and the medium in which he offers himself to God.[17]

---

14 Michael Novak, "Creation Theology," in *Co-Creation and Capitalism*, eds. John W. Houck and Oliver F. Williams, (Lanham: University Press of America, 1983), 28.

15 Henry, *Aspects of Christian Social Ethics*, 47.

16 Stevens, *Doing God's Business*, 5.

17 Dorothy Sayers, *Creed or Chaos*, (London: Methuen & Co., 1942), 53.

Sayers believes churches have adopted a view of work contrary to this one—a view that is pagan. I agree. For example, some Christians argue that the only reason they work is to provide for their families. They believe their work has no deeper value. Yet, Ryken reminds us of work's connection to creation: "The work of God, even though it is unique, remains a model for human work. It affirms that work is good and Godlike in principle."[18] "Human work has meaning because it expresses the divine image in people."[19]

Furthermore, it is estimated that one spends 11,000 days of his life at work; therefore, work not consciously consecrated as worship is a tragic loss. Sherman and Hendricks agree. "As humans, we act as junior partners in what is ultimately God's work. Yet participation in that work makes it our work, too. We are co-laborers with God in managing his creation . . . God chooses us to participate in his plans."[20] They go on to describe legitimate work as an extension of God's work. They write, "By legitimate work I mean work that somehow contributes to what God wants done in the world, and does not actively contribute to what he does not want done."[21]

Therefore, the laborer reflects the Creator's work in the midst of metal filings and toxic fumes. In fact, the Christian worker's confidence stands on God's unique portrayal of his image in each of their lives. What does that imply for our working lives? Haughey writes, "That image isn't up for grabs here. Here is a Creator who creates, produces, works—in a word, takes dominion. Here is a creature made in the image of this God to whom God gives dominion over what God has made. What could be clearer?"[22] Haughey continues, saying man is created to be creative with God's creation. "Putting form where there is formlessness is something we do every day. It might involve something as simple as straightening the desk or making the bed."[23]

---

18 Leland Ryken, *Work and Leisure in Christian Perspective*, (Portland: Multnomah, 1987), 122.

19 Ibid., 123

20 Doug Sherman and William Hendricks, *Your Work Matters to God*, (Colorado Springs: NavPress, 1987), 83.

21 Ibid., 84.

22 John C. Haughey, *Converting 9 to 5*, (New York: Crossroads, 1989), 33.

23 Ibid., 34.

Taking dominion prevents the world from reverting to chaos. This command has never been rescinded.[24]

Burns concurs: "At the same time that human beings share a common origin, each of us contributes a unique way of being and a particular mode of doing as an expression of our being."[25] Listen, for example, to the pride in crane operator Hub Dillard's words, quoted in *Working* by Studs Terkel.

> There's a certain amount of pride—I don't care how little you did. You drive down the road and you say, "I worked on this road." If there's a bridge, you say, "I worked on this bridge." Or you drive by a building and you say, "I worked on this building." Maybe it don't mean anything to anybody else, but there's a certain pride knowing you did your bit.[26]

God's first direct work of grace toward mankind was to create people in his own image. God is so vast and great that we each reflect aspects of him. Children of the same parents reflect this diversity. One is an achiever and justice seeker. Another is a dreamer and communicator. Still another is an artist and designer. Similarly, God equips his created image with diverse strengths, and the result is that individuals uniquely glorify him in their work. "Vocation is the divine invitation to self-realization according to this image, and is unique-singular-unrepeatable precisely because this image is inexhaustible."[27] Moreover, "Our potential for creative work is an essential part of our Godlike humanness, and without work we are not fully human. If we are idle (instead of busy) or destructive (instead of creative) we deny our humanity and so forfeit our self-fulfillment."[28]

---

24 Ibid., 35.

25 Burns, "The Call of Creation," 24.

26 Studs Terkel, *Working: People talk About What They Do All Day and How They Feel About What They Do,* (New York: Pantheon Books, 1972), 54.

27 Germain Grisez, *Personal Vocation,* (Huntington: Our Sunday Visitor Publishing, 2003), 80,81.

28 John Stott, "Reclaiming the Biblical Doctrine of Work," Christianity Today, May 4, 1979, quoted in Leland Ryken, *Work and Leisure,* 164.

CHAPTER 3

The Creator's Mandate

"Work," writes William Diehl, "refers to any human activity that cooperates with God's ongoing creation."[29] A laborer drives the large forklift through the muck after a rain storm. His boots and lower pant legs are caked with mud. For what seems like the one-hundredth time he climbs down from the cab and straightens the metal tubing that rests precariously on the forks. Today is Wednesday, and the weekend seems far away. His legs ache from continually climbing in and out of the cab, and the lead hand is yelling something about needing different pipe than the size he delivered minutes ago. Still, he cannot say he hates his work. On the contrary, he is challenged to keep a vast array of material organized. And he feels pride in the improvements he has made in the company's back lot. Sometimes he feels closest to God when he is bringing order to piles of tubing, pipe and angle iron.[30]

As he lifts and sorts steel, he feels satisfaction, because his work fulfills God's mandate to subdue the earth. "When we read in the first chapter of the Bible that man is to subdue the earth, we know that these words refer to all the resources contained in the visible world and placed at man's disposal. However, these resources can serve man only through work."[31]

---

29 William Diehl, *The Monday Connection*, (San Francisco: Harper, 1991), 29.

30 From a conversation with a welding shop worker

31 Pope Jean Paul II, *Laborem Exercens*, (Washington: Office of Publishing and Promotion Services, United States Catholic Conference, 1981), 25,26.

But humankind does not exist for the glory of work. As a case in point, the former Soviet Union glorified and perhaps deified work at the expense of workers' dignity. As a result, workers were demoralized and work quality deteriorated. Instead, work is to be in mankind's best interest. "In fact, in the final analysis it is always man who is the purpose of the work, whatever work it is that is done by man—even if the common scale of values rates it as the merest 'service,' as the most monotonous, even the most alienating work."[32]

Both Old and New Testaments present work as an environment where workers live in relationship to God. God put Adam and Eve in the Garden of Eden to work it; Abraham and Sarah were wealthy stock breeders; Joseph worked as a civil servant; Pharoah's court was the context for God's work; Peter, Andrew, James and John worked as fishermen; Paul continued as a tentmaker while he traveled and preached; Lydia was a businesswoman. Although Jesus' mediation between God and people is the primary theme in the New Testament, work is woven into this story in both the Old Testament and the New.[33]

Therefore, the challenge for blue-collar workers is the challenge all workers face: how can they experience faith in the context of work as much as they experience faith during a worship service? The answer, in part, is found in the Creator's mandate that his people should work. This truth can help workers realize God is interested in their jobs.

Moreover, their jobs involve active discovery of God's creative secrets. Pope Jean Paul II envisioned vocation as subduing the earth by discovering God's secrets. Once workers make discoveries, they turn their newly acquired knowledge into useful inventions.[34] Ryken notes, "By removing any stigma from the material world itself, the Christian doctrine of creation also takes away the reproach that other traditions have placed upon earthly work."[35]

---

32 Pope Jean Paul II, *Laborem Exercens*, 15.

33 Steve Jacobsen, *Hearts to God, Hands to Work*, (New York: The Alban Institute, 1997), 3.

34 Novak, "Creation Theology," 28.

35 Ryken, *Work and Leisure in Christian Perspective*, 122.

"The ideal is for a Christian to 'serve God in his work, and the work itself must be accepted and respected as the medium of divine creation.'"[36] God inspired Paul with the foundation for this truth:

> Slaves, obey your earthly masters in everything; and do it, not only when their eye is on you and to win their favor, but with sincerity of heart and reverence for the Lord. *Whatever you do,* work at it with all your heart, as working for the Lord, not for men, since you know that you will receive an inheritance from the Lord as a reward. It is the Lord Christ you are serving. (Colossians 3:22-24; italics added)

Therefore, work ought to be done to please God and improve people's lives. In other words, God gave people work for their own benefit, not for the benefit of work itself. Workers question this when the job is hard. "Anyone who has worked in any field knows the toil and suffering always involved in it—the teacher grading papers, the dentist probing mouths, the digger in a gravel pit, the miner, the preacher, the political leader on the telephone."[37]

One aspect of work as an instrument of blessing is its socially redeeming value. "While it may be true that any kind of work may have periods of intrinsic pleasure and interest—i.e., bricklaying, running a punch press, writing, painting,—nonetheless most work is not intrinsically fulfilling, but a necessity as social beings."[38]

Put succinctly, if you want to know what people are truly like, work with them for a while. The workplace has its own community, which is a significant motivation for workers either to give their best or to lose morale. This is an important part of fulfilling God's mandate to work.[39]

Linda's experience illustrates the social value of work. She was depressed, irritable and often engaged in fierce arguments with her

---

36 Dorothy Sayers, *Why Work*? (London: Methuen & Co., 1942), 56-60, quoted in Ryken, *Work and Leisure*, 174.

37 Novak, "Creation Theology, 19.

38 Stanley Hauwerwas, "Work as Co-Creation: A Critique of a Remarkably Bad Idea," in *Co-Creation and Capitalism*, eds. Houck and Williams, 48.

39 Joe Holland, *Creative Communion—Towards a Spirituality of Work*, (New York: Paulist Press, 1989), 11.

teenage daughter. Neither counseling nor other measures seemed to help. One day her husband noticed his wife's depression was lifting and her arguments with their daughter were less frequent. What made the difference? Linda had a new job at a busy drug store where she saw friends and acquaintances during the day. The new job gave her responsibility for a department and the work renewed her perspective. Her former job as an aide at a preschool had no longer satisfied her since she had been given little responsibility. "In short, the change in work had done what prayer, counseling, and her doctor could not do; give her a rewarding and meaningful activity."[40]

So work is not an end in itself; instead it is a gift from God and though labor does not provide material that workers take beyond the grave, God expects workers to find satisfaction in their work.

> Then I realized that it is good and proper for a man to eat and drink, and to find satisfaction in his toilsome labor under the sun during the few days of life God has given him—for this is his lot. Moreover, when God gives any man wealth and possessions, and enables him to enjoy them, to accept his lot and be happy in his work—this is a gift of God. He seldom reflects on the days of his life, because God keeps him occupied with gladness of heart (Ecclesiastes 5:18-20; cf. 3:13).

---

[40] Jacobsen, *Hearts to God, Hands to Work*, 42.

PART TWO

SIN INFECTED WORK

God created work, and he created workers in his own image. But through willful disobedience, humankind infected work with sin.

CHAPTER 4

The Worker's Rebellion

Sin corrupts workers

Adam and Eve introduced sin into the workplace when they rebelled against God. He revealed the consequences of their refusal to believe that his love was genuine: their unbelief poisoned their relationship with God, each other, and their work environment (Genesis 3:16-19). Their condition and ours became one contaminated by idolatry, hostility, jealousy, and selfish ambition (Galatians 5:19-21). Mouw describes sin's impact on the workplace as well as the entire world.

> . . . when Adam and Eve disobeyed God's commands a curse was introduced into the creation that apparently sent shock waves throughout the nonhuman realm: "cursed is the ground because of you . . . thorns and thistles it shall bring forth to you." (Gen. 3:17-18); and the Old Testament prophets view hostilities among the animals as a manifestation of sinfulness (see, e.g. Isa. 11:6-7).[41]

Adam and Eve rejected simple obedience, believing the lie that they would be like self-sufficient, independent gods.[42] Sin contaminated

---

41 Mouw, *Called to Holy Worldliness*, 34.

42 Leon Kass, *The Hungry Soul: Eating and the Perfecting of Our Nature*, (Chicago: University of Chicago Press, 1999), 208, 209, quoted in Paul Stevens, *Down to Earth Spirituality*, (Downers Grove: Intervarsity Press, 2003), 36.

everything, embedding patterns of cynicism and unbelief in the human psyche. So, the Christian laborer, who wants to honor Christ at work, may question how this is possible when a co-worker accuses him, using graphic, demeaning language, of cutting pipe the wrong length. A follower of Christ is tempted, in that instance, to give up the belief that work glorifies God. Christians who worship God with faith and hope on Sundays often feel worship is irrelevant during the work week. As a result, workers might opt for two separate worlds, one for the sacred and the other for secular day-to-day tasks, which they believe they cannot perform with grace and truth but only through force and deception.

Terkel, in his book *Working,* echoes this perspective on work.

> This book, being about work, is, by its very nature, about violence—to the spirit as well as to the body. It is about ulcers as well as accidents, about shouting matches as well as fistfights, about nervous breakdowns as well as kicking the dog around. It is, above all (or beneath all), about daily humiliations. To survive the day is triumph enough for the walking wounded among the great many of us.[43]

But the Bible does not describe work as cursed. Instead, it sees the source of workplace evil as emanating from within man.[44] So, workers are no longer in sync with the creation but struggle within it to do God's work. The broken inner life of the worker contributes to the broken morale of the workplace. The Apostle Peter counsels believers to "abstain from sinful desires which war against your soul." (1 Peter 2:11) Sin within the person taints the outer work.

Sin corrupts the workplace

Sin impacts the workplace as well as the workers. This is manifested, for example, through polarization of workers and management. Their relationship is often adversarial; they default to a position of mistrust. The greatest cause of workers' concern is often

---

43 Terkel, *Working,* xiii.

44 Kaiser, *Theology of Work,* 60.

not money but who they work with. Through this need for good working relationships, one sees loyalty to the crew as a significant factor in workers' satisfaction. For example, workers might stay on the job because of loyalty to their foreman, whom they perceive as one of their own, even though they hate the boss. Unfortunately, the boss reinforces their resentment when he accuses a laborer, who was injured on the job, of clumsiness.[45]

Resentment leads workers to completely separate work from the rest of their lives. For example, a worker may feel, "I don't want to be treated like an instrument. The result is that I *use* the work more than *do* the work. I have decided to have other fish to fry with the salary I receive."[46] As a result, workers turn inward and adopt the attitude that says, "I will retreat into my own self-interested world and milk the outside world for all it's worth (which, as far as I can see, isn't very much)."[47]

Workers, as well as managers, contribute to this polarization. One manifestation of workers' sin is the attitude that someone owes them a living. Katie, a perpetual welfare recipient, illustrated this attitude. She was a young woman who became pregnant in high school and subsequently entered a forced marriage with an alcoholic who beat her. After divorce and another abusive relationship, she turned to drugs. But she said welfare and food stamps also had an addictive impact. Thirty-three years after beginning her cycle of dependence on welfare, she managed to escape the pattern.[48]

Sin corrupts workers' relationship with creation

Another dimension of rebellion appears in workers' relationship with creation. Instead of taking care of the environment, workers, especially since the industrial revolution, have tended to use it as a limitless resource. This misplaced confidence in earth's ability to supply every want and need may substitute for faith in the living God. Perhaps this attitude is akin to Adam and Eve's belief that the fruit of the forbidden tree would give godlike ability. Therefore, instead

---

45 From a conversation with a laborer

46 John C. Haughey, *Converting 9 to 5*, (New York: Crossroads, 1989), 29.

47 Ibid., 31.

48 Charles Colson and Jack Eckerd, *Why America Doesn't Work*, (Dallas: Word, 1991), 77,78.

of subduing the earth as responsible earth-keepers, workers and technology pillage earth to satisfy growing appetites. This belief in the perpetual supply of the earth results in carelessness. Creation " . . . is not to rule man. However, there is a twistedness in humanity which causes us to perform such a task with fierce and destructive delight. Try as we might, we cannot subdue this."[49] Diehl agrees.

> Humankind certainly has multiplied and, in many respects, has subdued the earth. But "subdue" means to bring under control, not to destroy. As humankind grows in numbers and in technological sophistication, the danger increases that instead of controlling the earth we will rape it, deplete its resources, and pollute it to the point where it can no longer sustain life.[50]

Bernbaum adds, "Human beings were intended to subdue the earth for God's glory but instead sought to exploit it for themselves."[51]

---

49 John N. Oswalt, "kabash," in *Theological Wordbook of the Old Testament,* 1:430.

50 Diehl, *The Monday Connection,* 27.

51 John A. Bernbaum and Simon M. Steer, *Why Work? Careers and Employment in Biblical Perspective,* (Grand Rapids: Baker Book House, 1986), 9.

CHAPTER 5

The Workers' Judgment

The truck driver experiences the impact of human fallenness. His "swamper," who rides along, helps carry heavy gypsum into buildings, dislikes work, and smokes a joint while traveling between job sites. As a result, the driver has to find a way to motivate him while confronting him about illegal drug use at work. So, by evening, the driver arrives home exhausted; his dream of part-time evening studies is sidelined during a quick supper and sleep because the next morning at six o'clock, he will again be driving and unloading tons of material.[52] Why is his work, besides its tough physical dimension, so hard? Marshall answers, " . . . we should note that in Genesis the curse was not the imposition of labor as such but only that labor would become harsh and painful; it is clear that work was considered one of the blessings before the fall."[53] Genesis 3:16,17 reveals that, "Pain in childbirth ('issabon and eseb) are decreed for the woman (Genesis 3:16), and pain in manual labor ('issabone) is decreed for the man (Genesis 3:17). Both came as the consequence of the sin respecting the fruit of the forbidden tree."[54] Furthermore, the word "toil" in verse seventeen is also used in Isaiah 54:6 to describe the emotional anguish of a

52 Conversation with a truck driver, 2007.

53 Paul Marshall, "Vocation, Work, and Jobs", in *Labour of Love,* ed. Josina Van Nuis Zylstra, (Toronto: Wedge Publishing, 1980), 2.

54 Ronald B. Allen, "asab," in *Theological Wordbook of the Old Testament,* 2:688.

forsaken wife, in 2 Samuel 19:3 of a mourning father, in Isaiah 14:3 of exiled people and in Proverbs 15:13 of a broken spirit.[55]

Work became less and less pleasant and productive as workers moved further from God's revealed will, as this Old Testament example reveals:

> You will sow much seed in the field but you will harvest little, because locusts will devour it. You will plant vineyards and cultivate them but you will not drink the wine or gather the grapes, because worms will eat them. You will have olive trees throughout your country but you will not use the oil, because the olives will drop off (Deuteronomy 28:38-40).

And even the laborer who tries to follow Jesus in the marketplace might well echo the words of Ecclesiastes: "What does a man get for all the toil and anxious striving with which he labors under the sun? All his days his work is pain and grief; even at night his mind does not rest. This too is meaningless." (Ecclesiastes 2:22, 23) Work itself bears the judgment of sin because it is carried out in a sinful world by sinful people. "The Bible thus gives us two themes regarding work: First, as partners with God, we control and develop God's creation through our work. And second, because of our rebellious nature, we are destined to work hard and sweat in order to exist."[56]

Sin alienates workers from meaning

Work does not give meaning to life, no matter how hard one works. When one does not understand the situation of the worker in light of human sinfulness and its subsequent poisoning of work, one is left with a hopeless perspective. Weinberg illustrates this hopelessness,

> It is almost irresistible for humans to believe that we have some special relation to the universe, that human life is not just a more-or-less farcical outcome of a chain of accidents reaching back to the first three minutes . . . It is very hard to

---

55 Forrell and Lazareth, *Work as Praise*, 32.

56 Diehl, *The Monday Connection*, 27.

> realize that this [comfortable planet] is just a tiny part of an overwhelming hostile universe . . . The more the universe seems comprehensible, the more it also seems pointless.[57]

Even laborers who want to honor Christ are tempted to regard work itself as a curse. After sweeping iron filings and slag, listening to co-workers' foul language and perverse sexual references all day, the worker finds it difficult to see anything positive about his workplace. Furthermore, his growing willingness to return the crude insults he receives at work wear him down emotionally and spiritually.[58] Rather than believe work is simply a curse to endure, he needs to be reminded that work problems have spiritual roots. "Any drudgery or monotony or ordeal experienced at work can be traced to the original cleavage we call the Fall. Hassles take on a meaning beyond the here and now."[59]

Moreover, since the Industrial Revolution, workers have lost much of their identity in the wheels of industry. The age of systems and machines makes it harder to see how personal faith can integrate with work. As a result of sin, many workers experience work as nothing more than a means of survival. Even though work has a social dimension for the worker, he sees his workplace as a necessary evil. Hauerwas exposes the impact sin has on work; sin renders some work inhumane. He proposes that work's unpleasant but necessary character "forces us to discover and enhance those aspects of our lives that are not work."[60]

Workers are also alienated from their work when managers describe them as "assets" or "resources" that add value to the company. They can be acquired, trained, broken and discarded. But workers are created in God's image to do creative work. Holland says, " . . . human work needs to be judged by the criterion of conscious participation in the creative process."[61] But this is not often the case for the worker.

---

57 Steven Weinberg, *The First Three Minutes*, (New York: Basic Books, 1998), 154,155, quoted in Barbara Smith-Moran, *Soul at Work*, (Winona: Saint Mary's Press, 1997), 94.

58 Conversation with a laborer, 2007.

59 Haughey, *Converting 9 to 5*, 25.

60 Hauerwas, *Work as Co-creation*, 50.

61 Holland, *Creative Communion*, 40.

> Another way to put it is that we live in a materialistic society, where property and goods are deemed to be of the utmost importance—the more you have the better off you are. The problem with this kind of thinking is that it reduces man to being a servant of his economic needs or wants. It also makes a worker valuable only as long as he contributes to the production process and can't be replaced by a more efficient (cheaper) machine.[62]

A welding shop worker experienced something similar to this when his boss contemplated firing him because he had been injured a few times in a workplace that was devoid of safety precautions.[63]

Furthermore, when workers are seen only as "employees", they are easily dispensed with. "The structural sin of unemployment is a fundamental assault on human dignity. It denies the image of the Creator in the unemployed."[64] Although unemployment hurts workers, attempts to value workers have failed. "When a lot of labor is needed, the free market buys a lot. When a lot is no longer needed, the free market lets it go into unemployment. Then, if there are many extra workers, labor can be bought at a cheap price."[65] Marxism also failed miserably in its bid to offer dignity to the worker. "Rejecting the free market, it elevated the state as the organizing principle of the work process. But workers were still reduced to mechanistic forces of production."[66] Both capitalism and Marxism repress spirituality in the workplace, the former marginalized it while the latter repressed it.[67]

Therefore, economic systems are unable to remove the impact of sin in the workplace. And the result is an alienated and frustrated work force. A rather telling conversation with a plant worker, at his station on an automotive assembly line, went like this:

---

62 Ed Grootenboer, *About Work and Unions,* (London, Ontario: Christian Labour Association of Canada, 1984), 8.

63 From a conversation with a laborer.

64 Holland, *Creative Communion*, 13.

65 Ibid., 13

66 Ibid., 14.

67 Ibid.

> "Why do you work here?"
> "Oh, I need the money," he replied, his fingers and eyes working automatically at their repetitive task. "The pay is good. We get pretty good benefits too."
> "Alright, but does that mean you like your work here?"
> After a long stare, which even through his safety glasses showed his disbelief and astonishment at such a stupid question, he said,
> "Listen friend, anyone who says he likes his work is either lying through his teeth, or else he's plumb crazy."[68]

To many workers, work is mind numbing and soul starving.

> In many instances, particularly in manufacturing, but also in other sectors, employees are asked to do nothing more than to punch in, put in their eight hours and punch out. The results are frustration, a devil-may-care attitude, absenteeism, inferior workmanship, inefficiency, as well as untold social costs in the form of, for example, drug and alcohol abuse and family breakdowns.[69]

Other forces that resist a Christian perspective of work

Blue-collar workers encounter a great struggle when trying to maintain a biblical perspective on their work. Various forces resist their desire to see work as service to God and the common good. They also face legitimate fears of losing status, losing power, or being alienated because of their faith.

Seeking workplace status is one obstacle to a biblical perspective. Status-seeking is part of a condition sometimes called "careerism." This refers to seeing the job as a way to gain significance rather than an opportunity through which to serve God and people. Careerism is illustrated by this quote from a book on managing work life.

---

68 Grootenboer, *About Work and Unions*, 14.
69 Ibid., 20.

> Your career is a part of your life, your identity, a part of who you are and how you feel. For example, if you woke up tomorrow and your boss said, 'You're fired,' that would definitely upset your whole life. The fact that your career and your life are intertwined is one thing we must acknowledge when we face life's great challenges, such as divorce, the death of a family member, a personal illness or sick relative, even a pregnancy."[70]

Any legitimate career is a field of service to the Lord (Colossians 3:23), however, careerism is an attitude that exalts advancement or honor in one's field as a symbol of significance. Satan tempted Jesus to choose temporary advancement by worshiping Satan over worship of the living God, and in return Satan proposed to give Jesus all the kingdoms of the world and their splendor. Jesus sternly rebuked the devil, citing God's command to "Worship the Lord your God, and serve him only." (Matthew 4:8-10)

Careerism is not the same as advancement or financial success through work; instead, careerism mistakenly derives feelings of worth from one's status. The difference is subtle but it can be dangerous to spiritual health. The Apostle John issues this warning which can be applied to one's search for significance through career status. "Do not love the world or anything in the world. If anyone loves the world, the love of the Father is not in him. For everything in the world—the cravings of sinful man, the lust of his eyes and the boasting of what he has and does—comes not from the Father but from the world." (1 John 2:15, 16)

Moreover, blue-collar workers may not perceive their jobs as dignified service to God in part because they do not see their work as a legitimate response to God's call. Other factors faced by blue-collar workers include lower compensation than white-collar workers, shift work, more danger and hazards on the job, and less job security than white-collar counterparts.[71] "With regard to the five components of occupational status level (money, power, prestige, nature of the work, and amount of prerequisites, like education), blue-collar work clearly

---

[70] Robin Ryan, *What to Do with the Rest of Your Life,* (New York: Simon and Schuster, 2002), 5.

[71] Shostak, *Blue-collar Life,* 67-77.

earns a low ranking in the judgment of the general public."[72] Fear of losing power can also discourage workers from serving God. For example, in tough environments, Christian workers might want to retaliate against bullies. Furthermore, workers often feel powerless to solve the problems of their places of work. As a result, they might suppress their creativity and disconnect emotionally from their work. Workers may compensate for lack of creative input on the job by spending earnings on fads. So work loses significance as a means of developing the earth, community, and relationship with God.[73]

This form of alienation between work and worker is another powerful force in the blue-collar world. Workers experience alienation when they lack information about management decisions that directly affect them. And they are further alienated when they are ridiculed or refused acceptance because of their faith. This gap between spiritual-emotional wholeness and work has been nurtured in part by secular philosophy. Laura Nash believes theology and philosophy have "scorned the discussion of business for thousands of years." She continues,

> Even Aristotle, writing over two thousand years ago, first considered the business person as a possible topic for his work on applied ethics, then rejected the proposition outright on the grounds that the purposes and mentality of the vulgar merchant or mechanic were not sufficiently well-minded for serious moral analysis.[74]

Similarly, today believers often struggle with the perception that their faith has no place at work. Loss of status, loss of power, and fear of alienation hamper workers' perspectives of God's call to service.

The Church has often neglected the value of work

The Church, throughout history, also contributed to the current sense of futility workers experience. Some theology has judged the

---

72 Ibid., 54.

73 Holland, *Creative Communion,* 11.

74 Aristotle, Eudemian Ethics, I.IV.2, quoted in Laura Nash, *Good Intentions Aside,* (Boston: Harvard Business School Press, 1993), 24.

worker as irrelevant to God's most holy purpose. Thomas Acquinas and Augustine, for example, distinguished between the contemplative life and the active life. The former was oriented to eternal things while the latter was concerned with present life. The active life was necessary "but only the contemplative life was truly free."[75]

Karl Barth summarizes the theology of work in medieval Christianity: "According to the view prevalent at the height of the high Middle Ages [secular work] only existed to free for the work of their profession those who were totally and exclusively occupied in rendering true obedience for the salvation of each and all. There could be no question of 'calling' for Christians in other professions."[76] In other words, laborers existed to serve the clergy.

The Reformers, by contrast, valued work; but some of them misinterpreted 1 Corinthians 7:20: "Each one should remain in the situation which he was in when God called him." The Reformers' views of this text led Christians to view their roles as their calling.

> Luther often interchanged calling and social station . . . While Calvin was more open to changing work, he usually advised people to stay put unless they had "good grounds" and, hence, clearly related calling or vocation to a Christian's place in the social order and the economic division of labor.[77]

The Greek word "klesis" (calling), however, is not used elsewhere to refer to workers' stations in life. So why assign this meaning to 1 Corinthians 7? This text more likely refers to adhering to their calling to be Christians regardless of their work or marital status.[78] What hope does the blue-collar worker have amongst bullies, tasks that seem meaningless, and decisions driven by concern over dollars instead of human well-being?

---

75 Marshall, *Vocation, Work, and Jobs*, 8.

76 Ibid.

77 Ibid., 12,13.

78 Ibid., 13.

PART THREE

CHRIST REDEEMED WORK

Jesus Christ offers hope to workers and the workplace. Although sin has degraded God's image in workers and corrupted the workplace, Christ's Gospel redeems them. As a result, even in the presence of sin, redeemed workers may honor Christ through their work.

CHAPTER 6

Christ is the Redeemer of Work

What are the implications of redemption for workers?

> I simply argue that the cross be raised again at the centre of the marketplace as well as on the steeple of the church. I am recovering the claim that Jesus was not crucified in a cathedral between two candles, but on a cross between two thieves; on the town garbage heap; at a crossroad so cosmopolitan that they had to write his title in Hebrew and in Latin and in Greek . . . at the kind of place where cynics talk smut, and thieves curse, and soldiers gamble. Because that is where he died. And that is what he died about. And that is where churchmen should be and what churchmen should be about.[79]

God identifies with workers and their work

The Bible announces grace to workers. Workplace culture, by contrast, often expects people to obtain worth through achievement. But Christ affirms human worth by simply giving the gift of salvation. "A grace theology . . . proclaims that all people are subjects of God's love and, therefore, of infinite worth, altogether apart from who they are and what they have done."[80]

---

[79] MacLeod, *Only One Way Left*, 38.

[80] Tex Sample, *Blue-Collar Ministry*, (Valley Forge: Judson Press, 1984), 122.

In other words, Jesus does not approach workers as though he were an uncaring supervisor. Instead, Jesus, " . . . being in very nature God, did not consider equality with God something to be grasped, but made himself nothing, taking the very nature of a servant, being made in human likeness." (Philippians 2:6,7) The word "servant" in Philippians 2:7, translates the Greek "doulos," which referred to " . . . the ordinary worker in ancient society."[81]

Moreover, Mark 6:3 says Jesus' service included work as a "techton, an artisan, craftsman, or we would say carpenter."[82] *All* Christ's work was an act of service to God, including his miracles, his teaching, his carpentry and his death and resurrection. Consequently, when workers disconnect faith from the job site or assume ethical action is the only means of living faith at work, they miss this point: Christ's redemption includes their work, which becomes an act of service to God. Through Christ, God enters the efforts and skills of the worker. "Jesus does not treat us as a king would a subject, but rather as a servant does the one he has come to serve (John 13:2-14), as the beloved does his lover (John 15:9)."[83]

God makes the workplace an instrument of change

God sanctifies workers *through* their work. Philippians 2:12,13 is an example of this interplay between the worker's obedience and God's work in the worker: "Therefore, my dear friends, as you have always obeyed—not only in my presence, but now much more in my absence—continue to work out your salvation with fear and trembling, for it is God who works in you to will and to act according to his good purpose." This work of God influences Christian workers whether they work in the marketplace or manage households.[84] In other words, work is a context for holy living rather than a place that stifles workers' spiritual development.

---

81 Richardson, *The Biblical Doctrine of Work*, 29.

82 Ibid.

83 Marie Theresa Coombs, *Called by God*, (Collegeville: Liturgical Press, 1992), 27.

84 Paul Stevens, *The Other Six Days: Vocation, Work and Ministry in Biblical Perspective*, (Grand Rapids: Eerdmans and Vancouver: Regent Publishing, 1999), 116.

Just as a first century slave worked in an environment of ungodly influences, according to 1 Peter 2:21-24, a 21st Century laborer often does too. The worker who goes home filthy from dust and iron filings understands that he lives in a fallen world. Christ-centered living does not mean workers' contexts must be morally pure. Instead, "As new creatures in Christ, Christians are to have a Christ-centered orientation in life. This orientation has major implications for the way we work."[85] Even in difficult circumstances, God shapes workers' character as they work to please him. They need to reassess their attitudes toward work, when they are governed by resentment against their jobs, or by slavery to their work as a means of achieving status. The difficulties at work result from living in a fallen world, but one who wants to experience Christ's presence at work may look at these crises as a way of identifying with Christ's suffering.[86]

Simply put, God's presence in workers transforms their work into an instrument of change. In fact, through the job, he shapes holy people. In other words, products of work, including wages, ought not be the chief motives for getting up in the morning. Ultimately, one anticipates receiving rewards in the world to come for good work in the world today (Matthew 25:14-46; Colossians 3:24).[87] This does not mean work will cease to be when God renews the earth. Rather, the apocalyptic vision of Revelation 21:24,26 pictures the kings of the earth bringing their splendor and the glory and honor of the nations into the holy city.[88]

In contrast to Christ-centered living at work, note Sherman's description of work without God: "It is a treadmill. It is a dog's existence. It is vain, futile. It is skydiving without a parachute. Only in Christ will you find true and lasting significance. Only the work you do for Christ can give real meaning and a sense of impact."[89]

Sherman states that Christ-centered work fulfills the will of God because Christ is Lord of the workplace. He concludes, "You do

---

85 Bernbaum and Steer, *Why Work?* 10.

86 Ibid., 10..

87 Stevens, *The Other Six Days*, 117.

88 Ibid., 118.

89 Doug Sherman, *Keeping Your Head Up When Your Job's God You Down*, (Brentwood, TN: Wolgemuth & Hyatt, 1991), 54.

your work to please him, not to impress others."[90] The Apostle Paul similarly stated that we should not work primarily to please people but to please the Lord (Colossians 3:23, 24). Indeed, Jesus sees good work even when the supervisor or the client does not; the Lord, not the boss, ultimately rewards the faithful worker (Ephesians 6:8).[91]

So, work is God's instrument of spiritual growth and sanctification for workers who intentionally make Christ the center of their workplace. Sanctification implies completeness, wholeness, or fitness to fulfill a purpose, and holiness. Furthermore, sanctification includes both the process of maturity and the end goal of holiness.

Holy work is service-oriented instead of status-seeking. In Romans 8:18-23, partially quoted above, Paul pictures people who have begun new life through the transforming presence of God's Spirit. They humbly serve, while waiting on God to complete his work in them. Sample writes, "Such a vision has the potential to reverse the field of an achievement culture. The aim of life is no longer for each person to be number one, but for each person to contribute to the completion of self, community, and creation."[92]

God calls workers to the ongoing process of sanctification. Spiritual work includes partnering with God in one's sanctification, and the workplace is a key context for this. This work of ongoing sanctification is inseparable from work in the material world where believers work in the marketplace and manage households.[93]

God is present in the workplace even when he is not acknowledged

The Spirit of God is present, not only in the Christian community, but also in the world. Moreover, those who believe the Spirit works in the church but not the world should realize that mere theology cannot bar God from going to work.[94] Furthermore, the Christian laborer who views fellow workers as living a dog's existence is likely to regard them with lack of respect or, at best, pity. To counter this error, believers must recognize that the Spirit of God is present in

---

90 Ibid., 67.

91 Ibid.

92 Sample, *Blue-Collar Ministry*, 123.

93 Stevens, *The Other Six Days*, 116.

94 Miroslav Volf, *Work in the Spirit*, (New York: Oxford University Press, 1991), 80.

the workplace, even where there is a continuous barrage of smut, disrespect and danger. Workers need to know God's presence reaches beyond errant theologies of work that keep God as a recluse in the church but absent from the marketplace. Quoting Luther, Volf writes, " . . . human work is God's mask behind which he hides himself and rules everything magnificently in the world."[95]

God is not dependent on human cooperation in order to carry out his work. His Spirit is active in the world. For example, in Isaiah 37:5-13 the Lord announced that his decisions cause calamity amongst Judah's enemies.[96] The same Holy Spirit is present in the workplace and in the worshiping congregation; the difference is in the receptivity of the people.[97] This view is based, in part, on Revelation 21:26,27 which depicts the new Jerusalem: "The glory and honor of the nations will be brought into it. Nothing impure will ever enter it, nor will anyone who does what is shameful or deceitful, but only those whose names are written in the Lamb's book of life." These verses depict two different groups with opposing motives, yet God is nonetheless Lord of all the nations. The point is that God's Spirit works in the marketplace, though most do not acknowledge him. In fact, work may be an evangelist pointing a nonbeliever to acknowledge God. "The modern notion of the self-made person is an impossibility. But people can become partners with God, carrying on his delegated work. This attitude is encapsulated in Psalm 127:1: 'Unless the LORD builds the house, those who build it labor in vain.'"[98] Christ works in the marketplace even when he is unnoticed.

However, Luther's perspective of God's work in the world was not always helpful. He nurtured the perception of separation between the workplace and the Spirit's work; he distinguished between the soul and what he called the "outward man." The outward man, he said, remains the old man while the inner man becomes a new man through salvation."[99] In contrast to Luther's view, Jesus healed both physical and spiritual ailments. The kingdom of God broke into the world through Jesus' miracles. So, when God sent his Spirit to carry

---

95 Ibid., 99.

96 Ibid.

97 Miroslav Volf, *Work in the Spirit*, 118,119.

98 Ryken, *Work and Leisure*, 126.

99 Volf, *Work in the Spirit*, 103.

on Christ's work, he sent him to work, not only in the spirits of people, but in their whole beings. "Because the whole creation is the Spirit's sphere of operation, the Spirit is not only the Spirit of religious experience but also the Spirit of worldly engagement. For this reason it is not at all strange to connect the Spirit of God with mundane work."[100]

So, the Spirit of God comforts Christians at work with the awareness that He is present, even in difficult circumstances. Moreover, he is actively engaged with workers who may not even acknowledge his existence. As the psalmist wrote, "Where can I go from your Spirit? Where can I flee from your presence? If I go up to the heavens, you are there; if I make my bed in the depths, you are there. If I rise on the wings of the dawn, if I settle on the far side of the sea, even there your hand will guide me, your right hand will hold me fast." (Psalm 139:7-10) God is present and active in every workplace.

God changes the relationship between Christians and their work

How, then, does the sanctified Christian relate to work in the world? Before answering this, one needs to define "the world." First, "world" can refer to physical geography: "And this gospel of the kingdom will be preached in the whole world as a testimony to all nations, and then the end will come." (Matthew 24:14) Second, "the world" depicts a sinful environment. "To love the world," in this sense, is to attach oneself to things that are "transitory and illusory; it is to adopt the values of the sinful social order." [101] Finally, "the world" has a positive meaning. God loves the world (John 3:16). The Greek word translated "world" in John 3:16 is "*cosmos*, referring to the *created order*."[102] Moreover, Jesus came to save the world. "The creator God who judged his creation to be 'very good' at its beginnings (Gen. 1:31) has reaffirmed its fundamental worth by sending his son to renew it."[103] This third definition of "the world" is what we are concerned with.

Blue-collar Christians can fulfill God's creation mandate *in* his world, recognizing his redeeming love *for* the world. Therefore,

---

[100] Ibid., 104.

[101] Mouw, *Called to Holy Worldliness*, 33.

[102] Ibid., 34.

[103] Ibid.

workers embody God's holiness in the welding shop, the construction site, the hotel laundry room; they are saints of God—ministers of reconciliation at work. "God's aim is to reconcile all things in Christ. The gospel is the good news that God works for the redemption of the whole universe, that all things are to be united in Christ, and that each Christian has his own proper role to play in the accomplishment of this great goal (1 Corinthians 12; Ephesians 4:1ff)."[104]

In summary, redeemed blue-collar workers live in the presence and power of the Spirit of God at work. Work is both context and instrument for sanctification. Furthermore, the marketplace is a place where the Holy Spirit works in the hearts of unbelievers—a place where even unbelievers bring glory to God through work sanctioned by the Spirit of God. Finally, the workplace is a context for reconciliation through Christ with God, other people, and the work itself.

---

104 Henlee H. Barnette, *Christian Calling and Vocation*, (Grand Rapids: Baker, 1965), 21.

CHAPTER 7

Christian Workers Continue the Creation Mandate

Not only did Christ redeem workers and their work, he also reestablished the importance of God's mandate to subdue the earth. The following poem by Peter Terzick illustrates how blue-collar labor contributes to this mandate.

> I am a building tradesman. My hands are custodians of skills a thousand generations old, held in trust for a thousand generations. My predecessors created the Hanging Gardens of Nebuchadnezzar and patiently put together the Parthenon. My successors will construct platforms in space and way stations on the stars. I harness the rivers, bridge the inlets, disembowel the mountains, and level the valleys to make the nations strong in war and prosperous in peace. The mightiest skyscraper begins with a stake I drive in the ground and ends with the turn of the owner's key in a lock I install. Between the stake and lock I fight searing summer heat and bitter winter cold. Danger is my constant companion and instant death lurks around every corner. The astronaut begins his probe of the heavens from a launching pad I build. The mightiest surgeon performs his miracles in an amphitheater I erect and provide with heat, light, water, and technical equipment. Even at the birth of the atomic age one of my brothers* was there. And when

> the first test proved successful, Enrico Fermi, the master scientist, placed his arm around the shoulders of his brother and said: "Gus, with all our education, what could we have done without your experience?" I stand straight and walk proud, because I know my contribution to society is based on skill, not bluff; on sweat, not sweet-talk; on production, not press-agentry. I am a building tradesman, belonging to a building trades union. Because I am, I need truckle neither to king nor tycoon.
>
> *The first atomic reactor was built at the University of Chicago. The atomic pile was actually put together by Gus Kauth, a member of Carpenters Local No. 1922.[105]

Terzick's poem illustrates that blue-collar workers influence outcomes and their work carries on the creation mandate, even in a fallen world.

Work is still a gift from God

Scripture acknowledges work as God's gift and, therefore, something of value. For example, God inspired the author of Ecclesiastes to write,

> Then I realized that it is good and proper for a man to eat and drink, and to find satisfaction in his toilsome labor under the sun during the few days of life God has given him—for this is his lot. Moreover, when God gives any man wealth and possessions, and enables him to enjoy them, to accept his lot and be happy in his work—this is a gift of God. (Ecclesiastes 5:18,19)

However, many blue-collar workers perceive work as a necessary evil. Work seems satisfying to them only if the job presents challenges such as "achievement, responsibility, growth advancement, and earned

---

105 Peter Terzick, "I am a Building Tradesman," in *Of Human Hands*, ed. Gregory F. Augustine Pierce (Minneapolis: Augsburg, 1991), 47,48.

recognition."[106] Furthermore, most blue-collar workers see work as a means of affording things or of achieving a successful lifestyle.[107] For example, a young waitress might add up her tip total after work. If she had a profitable shift, she would be closer to her goal of having enough money to buy a car even as she saves money for an education she hopes will lead to better job opportunities.

Although these are legitimate motives for employment, they eclipse the greater vision of work as worship. Workers may treat work as a reality they must somehow cope with, while seeing faith as an ideal they must shield from contamination by their jobs. But, "According to Scripture you go to work for the same reason you go to church, to worship and serve Jesus Christ."[108]

Work is an expression of Christ's lordship

This service to Jesus Christ, the Lord of the workplace, furthers the creation mandate to subdue the earth through his servants. But the idea of keeping Christ central at work sometimes baffles workers. For example, how does a waitress remain Christ-centered even as she endures innuendo from men old enough to be her grandfathers? The church must remind her that Jesus also lived in real world settings among fishing boats, docks, fields, homes and the public square. Yet, in the most gritty environments, Jesus kept his Father's will central.

Jesus challenged work settings by his life and teaching. "Increasingly, Jesus confronted the institutions that existed more to be served than to serve. His arrival in Jerusalem is marked by turning over the money changers' tables and publicly ridiculing the religious authorities."[109] As well, Jesus dignified work by using the tools of his trade; workers ought not see the quality work of their hands as placing a barrier between their hearts and God.[110]

So, one would affirm that Jesus not only brought salvation to humanity, but that he also carried out the creation mandate as a responsible worker in daily life. Similarly, Christians in the workplace

---

106 Shostak, *Blue-collar Life*, 59.
107 Ibid., 60.
108 Sherman, *Keeping Your Head Up*, 60.
109 Jacobsen, *Hearts to God, Hands to Work*, 20.
110 Henry, *Aspects of Christian Social Ethics*, 52.

carry out God's creation mandate even as they live with the tension of being both aliens *and* citizens in the world.

Nobody said God's mandate would be easy

Jesus predicted his followers, as aliens in the world, would experience opposition: "If the world hates you, keep in mind that it hated me first. If you belonged to the world, it would love you as its own. As it is, you do not belong to the world, but I have chosen you out of the world. That is why the world hates you." (John 15:18,19) But even though he considered his followers aliens in the world, Jesus expected them to engage in the business of living in the world. He prayed, "As you sent me into the world, I have sent them into the world." (John 17:18)

Jesus illustrated the difficulty of following him when he told a parable describing God's kingdom. An enemy came in the night and sowed weeds throughout the crop. When the wheat grew up, so did the weeds; obviously, an enemy had been at work. But the land owner told his servants not to pull the weeds before the wheat matured because doing so would destroy the good plants (Matthew 13:24-30).

Workers face similar dilemmas. They might prefer a world defined by clear rules with consequences, a place where good is immediately rewarded and evil renounced or punished. Yet, like the world of the disciples, the workplace world consists of good mingling with evil. As a result, uprooting the weeds before harvest would destroy the crop.[111]

Therefore, Jesus affirms Christians' roles in the workplace because, though it is a fallen world, Christ has come to live, die and rise again in and for this world. As a result, workers further God's creation mandate by patiently improving the workplace, even when they feel alienated in this world.

Christian workers bring grace to a broken creation

God's workers, as part of the created order, bring healing to this wounded world. Although sin mars God's creation, grace nurtures

---

111 Thomas H. Green, *Darkness in the Marketplace: The Christian at Prayer in the World,* (Notre Dame, IN: Ave Maria Press, 1981), 11.

creation's healing.[112] The Christian, empowered by God's grace, is an agent of that healing.

The Bible directs Christians as to how they should respond to this healing grace. For example, 1 Peter 2:4,5 describes Christians as living stones who are being built up into a spiritual house to be a holy priesthood. This means they are God's agents in both work and culture. Therefore, Sherman and Hendricks call workers "a new clergy," and say pastors are responsible to "produce and equip the new clergy."[113]

Furthermore, the Christian's work nurtures faith in God, who infiltrates *every* aspect of life. Succinctly put, the work of God is to believe (John 6:29; Phil. 2:13; 2 Thess. 1:11),[114] and belief, to be credible, cannot be restricted to life at church. Instead, God gives work as a gift of grace with the result that workers redistribute his grace. "We receive everything from the Lord (1 Cor. 4:7), and somehow in the divine purpose God receives from us. In some mysterious way we enhance the glory of God . . . God is receptive to our love and to us because God wills it so."[115] In other words, God, purely through his grace, gives a person his work and, in turn, receives the work as praise. Although work does not make workers right with God, Christians influence a healthy workplace by their good work. "Paul here sees daily work as a sphere where one has positive contact with the world. It is a service to God and others while awaiting the day of the Lord . . . (1 Cor. 7:29-31)."[116]

Paul's work is another example of grace in the workplace. According to 1 Corinthians 9:19-23, the apostle worked so as not to be a burden to others. Moreover, it appears his work was sometimes part of his suffering (2 Cor. 11:23,27). In spite of the challenges, his dedication to work contrasted with those in Thessalonica who stopped work because they believed Christ's coming was imminent (2 Thess. 3:6-15). Paul countered their erroneous belief that work was not necessary. Furthermore, he said they should work to sustain themselves and that they should not give up doing good. Instead,

---

112 Holland, *Creative Communion*, 31.

113 Sherman and Hendricks, *Your Work Matters to God*, 216.

114 Richardson, *The Biblical Doctrine of Work*, 29.

115 Coombs, *Called by God*, 25.

116 Forrell and Lazareth, *Work as Praise*, 40.

believers are to work for God's glory in *everything* (2 Thess. 3:10; cf. Gen. 3:17-19).[117]

But was Paul referring to blue-collar work? When he referred to work, it is not always clear whether he was thinking of labor or apostolic ministry. "For him all the different types of work originated in faith. The work he considered was not limited to liberal pursuits; in fact, it was manual labour which most often drew his attention."[118] Marshall continues, "Even compared to the Stoic philosophers, who were the most generous in their appraisal of necessary work, the biblical authors stand out starkly in their praise of even the humblest honest labour. The Bible was a radical document in respect of work."[119] Paul sees Christian workers as instruments of God's grace in the world. Moreover, their work, done well, brings healing grace into the workplace.

Christian work brings dignity to the workplace

When a laborer spends all day sorting oil-soaked, dirt-encrusted bolts, he might believe that, like the Stoics, his body is a source of bondage, and work is a necessary evil. But the filth of the bolt bin is not his greatest concern; the filthy names some co-workers call him grind like iron filings through his thoughts. In order to keep his sense of spiritual direction, he needs continual renewal for his mind. Peter's inspired words can encourage him: "His divine power has given us everything we need for life and godliness through our knowledge of him who called us by his own glory and goodness. Through these he has given us his very great and precious promises, so that through them you may participate in the divine nature and escape the corruption in the world caused by evil desires." (2 Peter 1:3,4) Blue-collar Christians need to rely on divine power to live godly lives.

Reflecting grace and dignity at work is a more likely outcome if one believes that mundane tasks have a God-ordained purpose. Hugh Latimer, the early Puritan said,

---

117 Ibid.

118 Marshall, "Vocation, Work, and Jobs", 3.

119 Ibid., 6,7.

> Our Saviour Christ before he began his preaching . . . was a carpenter, and got his living with great labor. Therefore let no man disdain . . . to follow him in a . . . common calling and occupation. For, as he blessed our nature with taking upon him the shape of man, so in his doing, he blessed all occupations and arts.[120]

Ryken adds, "Work can be redeemed, even in a fallen world. Anything that helps us to overcome the effects of sin on work is part of this redemption. Work itself retains some of the quality of a curse, but the attitude of the worker can transform it."[121]

Consumers might regard blue-collar work as mundane, meaningless and undignified. To counter this view, Sherman and Hendricks describe the use of pallets built by their friend's company. While obscure, the pallets provide a mobile platform for things like grapefruit, cereal and milk containers, all of which end up on the breakfast table. Among the people contributing to this breakfast,

> . . . we should remember the trucks and their drivers that God has used to haul this food our way. And we should appreciate the truck stop operators along the way who have provided diesel fuel and coffee. And, of course, someone had to lay down those miles of interstate that connect our country. And finally, we should thank God for the supermarket employees, for the guy who carries the bag to our car, and for my wife who puts it all on the table.[122]

God's mandate to work brings dignity to the obscure workplace.

One concludes that all legitimate work glorifies God. Scripture affirms this as follows: "So whether you eat or drink or whatever you do, do it all for the glory of God." (1 Corinthians 10:31) Paul also affirmed the dignity of workers when he wrote to Titus, "Remind the people to be subject to rulers and authorities, to be obedient, to

---

120 H. M. Robertson, *Aspects of the Rise of Economic Individualism*, (New York: Kelly and Millman, 1959), quoted in Ryken, *Work and Leisure in Christian Perspective*, 134.

121 Ryken, *Work and Leisure in Christian Perspective*, 131.

122 Sherman and Hendricks, *Your Work Matters to God*, 88,89.

be ready to do whatever is good . . ." (Titus 3:1) The Bible features a variety of work that brings honor to God, as the following examples show: plowing by an anointed king--"Just then Saul was returning from the fields, behind his oxen . . ." (1 Samuel 11:5), shepherding by a young man soon to be anointed king--"He chose David his servant and took him from the sheep pens; from tending the sheep he brought him to be the shepherd of his people Jacob of Israel his inheritance . . ." (Psalm 78:70, 71), skilled craftsmanship by a tribesman--"Then the LORD said to Moses, 'See, I have chosen Bezalel son of Uri, the son of Hur, of the tribe of Judah, and I have filled him with the Spirit of God, with skill, ability and a knowledge in all kinds of crafts . . ." (Exodus 31:1-3), gate keeping by Levites--"The gatekeepers had been assigned to their positions of trust by David and Samuel the seer (1 Chronicles 9:22c)." [123] Droel and Pierce add: "All Christians should recognize . . . that they have a vocation, or calling, to Christian service, which can be carried out in a variety of ways and situations. One legitimate way of serving is certainly in institutional church programs. But that is not the only way."[124] In other words, to serve God in any capacity is honorable work.

Perhaps the greatest assault to workers' dignity is the persistent, impersonal repetition of the assembly line. However, the Bible provides a footing for meaningful service, even in monotonous contexts like assembly lines. Christ's followers, who work on assembly lines should regard themselves as participants in the company of God's royal servants. In the end, they will stand with all who have faithfully served the King of kings. Revelation 5:10 says of *all* faithful believers, "You have made them to be a kingdom and priests to serve our God, and they will reign on the earth." Thus, in God's overview of life, service to God in Christ's name gives meaning to otherwise mundane work.

Christian workers are called to be servants of the Lord no matter what their work is like. Work on an assembly line or a similar scenario does not alter the truth that a Christian is a child of God. Because of this, the Christian worker has a sense of purpose that an unbeliever cannot fathom.

---

123 Ryken, *Work and Leisure in Christian Perspective*, 132.

124 William L. Droel and Gregory F. Augustine Pierce, *Confident and Competent*, (Notre Dame, IN: Ave Maria Press, 1987), 35,36.

> If one is truly a believer, no boss and no machine can pluck him out of Christ's hand and thrust him into a morass of meaninglessness. Even monotony can be justified in the ministry of God and of humanity, if it stems from a constructive activity that has no better alternative. Whatever contributes to the elevation and good of mankind is worthy, even if it lacks romance and novelty.[125]

Even the most mundane work done by the most profane worker retains a measure of dignity because work is God's mandate. Christ as well as Old and New Testament witnesses affirm its value.

Christian workers redeem the work itself

During the 1960s, protests against tradition included an attack on the work ethic. Protesters believed freedom from work would improve the lot of people, however, God did not design people to avoid work. Instead, he created them to work and redeemed them to redeem work.[126]

For blue-collar Christians, therefore, work is a means of intentional service to God. What's more, work helps laborers express their faith in practical ways. A man who retired from the trucking industry illustrated the redemption of work in his workplace. He lamented that after only eighteen months of retirement, he sometimes felt useless. For nearly half a century, he worked in the industry, rising early and solving problems until evening. Correctly, he believed that his job was a significant field of service to the Lord and to people. He valued the sense of purpose associated with working and the community of his workplace. This is so even though there were aspects of the job he was glad to leave behind. The industry recognized him for his workmanship and stellar character, honoring him as "Dispatcher of the Year" for all of Canada.[127] His testimony illustrates this admonition to the believers: "Make it your ambition to lead a quiet life, to mind your own business and to work with your hands, just as we told you, so that your daily life may win the respect of outsiders and so that

---

125 Henry, *Aspects of Christian Social Ethics*, 59.

126 Colson and Eckerd, *Why America Doesn't Work*, 45.

127 Conversation with a trucking dispatcher, 2007.

you will not be dependent on anybody." (1 Thessalonians 4:11,12) As Carl Henry puts it,

> According to the scriptural perspective, work becomes a way-station of spiritual witness and service, a daily-traveled bridge between theology and social ethics. In other words, work for the believer is a sacred stewardship, and in fulfilling his job he will either accredit or violate the Christian witness.[128]

Christian blue-collar workers also redeem their workplaces through loving other people on the job. If they see peers and clients as beings created in God's image, they are more likely to value them as persons and love them in spite of their differences. Without a clear theology of creation, fall and redemption, they might see work as a waste of time, or as a necessary evil, and despise those they work with. "Without question, far too many workers (and customers) work from self-seeking, greedy motives. They cheat, they steal, they lie, they over-charge, they defraud, they rig the system. But these are sins of people, not flaws inherent in work."[129] Scripture teaches that even though sin has stained and twisted people and workplaces, God still intends work to be good.

Yet, in a sinful world, Christian often feel God's glory is crowded out at work. As a result, they feel their work is inferior to pastoral ministry or missionary service. For example, "A woman in a workshop on ministry apologized: 'You see, I've never had time to do ministry . . . I've never had time to do Altar Guild, teach the children in the school.' This woman was startled to realize that ministry included her work in the world: 'You mean looking after my mother for the last 20 years is part of my ministry?'"[130] Similarly, Holland describes work as an expression of God's love: "Work is a fundamental cultural way by which we reveal God's actively creative love . . . How imbalanced then to suggest today that only certain works are religious. Or that work is a distraction from knowing God. Or that work is a curse from sin.

---

128 Henry, *Aspects of Christian Social Ethics*, 31.

129 Sherman, *Keeping Your Head Up*, 183.

130 Droel and Pierce, *Confident and Competent*, 35.

Or that work is only a means for buying things."[131] Christian workers redeem work by treating it with dignity and diligence.

Christian workers can love God through their jobs

Some who enter career ministry, believing they have heard God's call to leave their jobs and enter pastoral ministry, become discouraged when they learn that career ministry is also a job. Pastoring is hard work that often yields few measurable results. Furthermore, pastors do not feel more holy than they did when they worked in the marketplace. They are the same people after they don the title of "pastor" or "missionary". Stevens writes, "What makes work God-blessed is not that God's Word and name are spoken out loud but that the work is done with faith, hope and love."[132] Scripture says, "Whatever you do, work at it with all your heart, as working for the Lord, not for men, since you know that you will receive an inheritance from the Lord as a reward." (Colossians 3:23-24)

> Everything about you is to be involved in loving God. It makes sense that your work must be involved as well. Just think about how much of your heart, soul, and might go into your work. Imagine, then, as you spend yourself at that task, being able to say, "I'm here to do something God wants done, and I intend to do it because I love Him." The person who can make this statement has turned his work into one of his primary means of obeying the greatest of God's commandments.[133]

Blue-collar workers should not quit their jobs when they feel that a career ministry role would be more pleasing to God. Instead, they should seek satisfaction *at* work through loving God *through* their work.

At the same time, believers need to know that loving God does not result in a continual, sublime awareness of God's deepest purpose in every task. William Diehl describes how he struggled to feel God's

---

131 Holland, *Creative Communion*, 36.

132 Stevens, *Down to Earth Spirituality*, 100.

133 Sherman and Hendricks, *Your Work Matters to God*, 94.

presence selling steel or in the office of a customer. "Yet," he writes, "just because we do not see something, it does not mean that is it not there."[134] Diehl shares his struggle to bring faith and work together.

> During my morning prayer time, I consider my agenda for the day and pray that I will be open to God's action in these events. I must confess that when things get rolling during the day, I usually forget to ask myself, "Where is God in all this activity?" Not until later do I reflect on whether I was aware of God's presence in the events of my day. Most of the time the answer is "No".[135]

Yet, sometimes God seems to break through, and at other times the impact of faith is not clear. Diehl describes a grueling nine hour negotiation, during which he represented a client who was buying a company from an unscrupulous seller. After six hours of negotiation, he walked to the window and looked down thirteen stories on the sun-drenched Boston harbor, questioning the presence of God. But the next morning he met with his client and three employees from the company his client had purchased. They were relieved that the new owner had purchased the company and they related terrible stories of what it had been like to work for the previous employer. After hearing from the employees, the vice president of the company noted that it was holy week and that the company had experienced something like a resurrection. Diehl writes,

> I was a bit shocked to hear this simile, but one of the new employees quickly came back with, 'Yeah, you know, you're right. I feel like the stone has just been rolled away!' There it was, and I had been too blind to see it. What had been going on in those nine hours of hard negotiations was the rescue of jobs and a new chance for some mighty fine people. We had secured their jobs and their pensions and given them a new future under a much better owner.[136]

---

134 Diehl, *The Monday Connection*, 28.

135 Ibid., 35.

136 Ibid, 35-37.

Although Diehl had not felt the presence of God at work that day, God was there, solving a seemingly impossible problem.

This feeling of God's absence from the workplace is even more pronounced for blue-collar workers, who seldom influence the management decisions that affect their lives. Workers often remain alienated from management. Therefore, blue-collar workers need encouragement from their churches. They need to know that their jobs are significant avenues through which they serve and love God. Christians in the workplace need to hear that they improve life for others. In other words, they work in partnership with God, not as equals but as co-workers.

In summary, Christ is the redeemer of work, and redeemed blue-collar workers continue his creation mandate. Although their role as God's co-workers is not an easy one, Christian workers bring grace, dignity, redemption and love to their jobs. By God's grace, they work in partnership with his Spirit to improve their world. Marshall summarizes,

> Our calling is to obediently serve in the healing, renewing, and unfolding of God's good creation; to love God, to live before his face in praying, raising children, doing justice, making chairs, building, playing, eating, sleeping; to do all things to his honor and glory. In doing this, we need to distinguish between those things which are the result of sin and those which reflect God's good creation, no matter how broken.[137]

---

137 Marshall, "Vocation, Work and Jobs," 15,16.

CHAPTER 8

God Calls Workers to a Relationship with Christ

What distinguishes the work of Christ's followers from others' work? To answer this question, one must explore the meaning of God's call in the life of the Christian worker. What *is* God's call? Stevens explains the terminology: "The English word vocation comes from the Latin word vocatio, which means calling; they are the same thing, though this is not obvious to people who use these words."[138]

God calls workers to himself

God calls workers into an on-the-job relationship, even when their jobs are frustrating. Earlier, I referred to a waitress, who takes flak from customers and whose co-worker takes more than her share of the tips. Like other workers, this waitress needs assurance that God has called her to a relationship with himself through Christ.

> As Christians, ours is a total calling to discipleship in the body of Christ (Rom. 1:7), to citizenship in the kingdom of God (1 Thess. 2:12), and to salvation (Rom. 11:29). The choice of a career therefore does not involve the search for a separate, distinct calling, but should be seen as an

[138] Paul Stevens, "Calling/Vocation," in *The Marketplace Ministry Handbook*, eds. Paul Stevens and Robert Banks. (Vancouver: Regent College Publishing, 2005), 33.

> important part of our response to the all-encompassing call of God to salvation."[139]

The call to salvation invites the worker to a relationship with God who has chosen her. As a result of God's call, she has become a full-time worker in his kingdom.

God's calling to a relationship with him is his initiative—his choice. The Apostle Paul encourages waitresses and all workers by reiterating his experience of being chosen by God: "In him we were also chosen, having been predestined according to the plan of him who works out everything in conformity with the purpose of his will, in order that we, who were the first to hope in Christ, might be for the praise of his glory." (Ephesians 1:11) God sent Christ to fulfill an eternal purpose and man had no say in this decision.[140] The fact that a waitress's work is frustrating does not diminish God's calling on her life; her job will not limit God's ability to carry out his purpose in her life.

Nemeck and Coombs conclude, "We select something because it strikes us as favorable, good or worthy. Divine election, on the other hand, transcends and sometimes defies all logic. The Lord selects uniquely out of love."[141] As a case in point, Moses preached,

> The LORD did not set his affection on you and choose you because you were more numerous than other peoples, for you were the fewest of all peoples. But it was because the LORD loved you and kept the oath he swore to your forefathers that he brought you out with a mighty hand and redeemed you from the land of slavery, from the power of Pharoah king of Egypt. (Deut. 7:7,8)

Furthermore, in the New Testament, the Greek word "kalein" is used almost two hundred times to refer to the believer's calling.

---

139 Bernbaum and Steer, *Why Work*? 12.

140 Jacobs and H. Krienke, "protithami," in *The New International Dictionary of New Testament Theology*, vol. 1, ed Colin Brown. (Grand Rapids: Zondervan, 1975), 697.

141 Coombs, *Called by God*, 40.

This word refers to God's call to receive his salvation (Romans 8:30; 1 Thessalonians 2:12, II Timothy 1:9).[142]

God, by his own gracious choice, calls the Christian worker to himself, and his call to blue-collar workers is a full-time calling. God's call to work in his kingdom cannot be part-time because he does not call the worker to a part-time relationship with him. Therefore, Ephesians 1:4-11 relates calling to our all-encompassing relationship with God. As a result, one's calling cannot be limited to one job in one place and time.

Rather, the message of the Gospel is that God calls people to peace and reconciliation with himself. So God's calling comes from his deep love, his undeserved favor or grace toward us. Paul used the illustration of Jacob and Esau to point out that God's blessing on Jacob was due entirely to God's grace rather than merit on Jacob's part. Commenting on this principle, Romans 9:12 says that God's purpose stands "not by works but by him who calls . . ." Thus, the Bible says the gospel is the gateway to God's call. Paul wrote about this to his friends: "He *called you to salvation* when we told you the Good News; now you can share in the glory of our Lord Jesus Christ." (2 Thess. 2:13b,14; NLT, italics added) In other words, God calls to new life those who receive his grace through Jesus. This calling is a miraculous, spiritual work of God in which God " . . . calls things that are not as though they were." (Rom. 4:17)

Furthermore, God's call to a relationship with himself demands a decision on the part of the one called. God's call is more than a mere invitation; it can be disobeyed, but once obeyed, God's call becomes his *claim* on one's life. God boldly laid claim to the Israelites when he declared, in Isaiah 43:1-3a,

> But now, O Israel, the LORD who created you says, "Do not be afraid, for I have ransomed you. *I have called you by name; you are mine.* When you go through deep waters and great trouble, I will be with you. When you go through rivers of difficulty, you will not drown! When you walk through the fire of oppression, you will not be burned up, the flames will not consume you. For I am the LORD your God, the Holy One of Israel." (italics added)

---

142 Barnette, *Christian Calling and Vocation*, 18.

As these verses imply, calling can include hardship and suffering. Therefore, God's call to relationship also includes his compassion and his care. God calls people to thorough devotion in a relationship where he saves, leads, and cares for those who respond by faith. One concludes then, that the effect of God's call is a changed heart and direction, not a changed career.

God calls the Christian waitress, through his grace, into a full-time relationship with himself and into full-time kingdom work. Thus, he calls her to experience his grace in the workplace. And that calling shapes character, influences personality and governs how one carries out her work.

The call is not synonymous with a job. Instead, calling remains constant when workers change jobs. And calling transcends specific kinds of employment with the result that workers can live faithfully for Christ regardless of the kind of work they do.[143]

143 Don Flow, "A Business Owner's Mission," in *Faith Goes to Work*, ed. Robert J. Banks, (New York: The Alban Institute, 1993), 69.

CHAPTER 9

God Calls Workers to Community

Christian workers bring community to the workplace

God calls workers to community with each other; he calls them to *be* the church. The church consists of those God has called to declare his glory everywhere, including the job site. Scripture declares, "But you are a chosen people, a royal priesthood, a holy nation, a people belonging to God, that you may declare the praises of him who called you out of darkness into his wonderful light." (1 Peter 2:9) As God's priesthood, Christian workers infuse community into their work world, bringing an attitude of reconciliation to their work.

Christian workers are God's priests in the workplace. But rather than lead ceremonies, they bring God's presence into their work by participating as servants in their work communities.

> We are called to peoplehood, not to point to ourselves, but to show forth the wonderful deeds of him who called us out of darkness. To be God's priestly people is to give our lives to the service of the needy and oppressed. To be a holy nation is to aid in delivering prisoners from their captivity. To be a chosen race is to refuse to claim any "purity" except the purity of Jesus' blood.[144]

---

144 Mouw, *Called to Holy Worldliness*, 45.

Priestly work is usually subtle. For example, a church member, whose work includes welding and drafting, shared how he was able to serve his boss and fellow workers, because the manager placed him in a position where he could maximize his gifts and bless the company. While some church officials might not view welding as priestly service, this Christian is known for caring about co-workers as well as caring for his work. He does so because he is aware of his calling as God's worker.[145]

Closely related to the priestly function of Christians is the ministry of reconciliation. God called those who were once far away in order that they will help others toward reconciliation with God and people.

> The ministry of reconciliation, however, is not limited to bringing men to God, but extends to the reconciliation of workers with workers. Moreover, all economic, social, and political ideologies are to be captured for Christ. Paul was ready to meet and to take "every thought [ideology] captive to obey Christ" (2 Corinthians 10:5). For in Christ "all things were created, in heaven and on earth, visible and invisible, whether thrones or dominions or principalities or authorities—all things were created through him and for him." (Colossians 1:16)[146]

Reconciliation is a vital aspect of priestly ministry at work because conflict is a regular occurrence in the workplace.

Christian workers bring community to the workplace. They do this as God's representative priests whose liturgy is their consistent, humble service. And they offer community at work through modeling the ministry of reconciliation.

Pastors nurture community among blue-collar workers

What role do pastors fill in workplace ministry if non-pastors are the key to ministry in the marketplace? In short, pastors prepare Christians to integrate biblical truth with workplace issues. When

---

145 Conversation with a draftsman, 2008.

146 Barnette, *Christian Calling and Vocation*, 20,21.

pastors prepare to preach, they might consider how the biblical sermon text applies to a workplace context. In particular, their teaching should affirm workers' calling to community. Moreover, pastors can help shape church life so that community is a priority. Finally, pastors themselves offer community to blue-collar workers.

Pastors have firm biblical authority to affirm workers as God's called people. For example, the Bible teaches equal standing of clergy and laity before God.

> Both *kleros* (from which is derived the word "clergy") and *laos* (from which comes "laity") denote the same persons in the New Testament. Two passages make this fact clear. Paul speaks of the church as the temple of the living God who declares: "I will live in them . . . and I will be their God, and they shall be my people [*laos*]" (ll Corinthians 6:16). And Peter exhorts elders (pastors) not to be "domineering over those in your charge [*kleros*]," but to be "examples to the flock" (1 Peter 5:3). Here both *kleros* and *laos* apply to the same people, the people of God, the whole church.[147]

Therefore, the called community is comprised of the whole church, including welders, mechanics, truckers and servers as well as teachers, executives and pastoral staff. However, blue-collar workers often feel less called than pastors or white-collar Christians. Pastors can influence blue-collar Christians to believe that God has called them to serve him through their work. Sayers argues, "It is not right for [the Church] to acquiesce in the notion that a man's life is divided into the time he spends on his work and the time he spends in serving God. He must be able to serve God in his work, and the work itself must be accepted and respected as the medium of divine creation."[148]

Pastors have unparalleled opportunities, through preaching and teaching, to encourage Christians in the workplace. Preachers could periodically apply sermons to workplace situations and issues, thereby demonstrating that blue-collar workers are intrinsic, important members of God's called community. Sayers asks, "Can anyone

---

147 Barnette, *Christian Calling and Vocation*, 34.

148 Sayers, *Creed or Chaos*, 56.

remain interested in a religion which seems to have no concern with nine-tenths of his life?"[149]

> The Apostles complained rightly when they said it was not meet they should leave the word of God and serve tables; their vocation was to preach the word. But the person whose vocation it is to prepare the meals beautifully might with equal justice protest: It is not meet for us to leave the service of our tables to preach the word.[150]

In addition to teaching blue-collar workers of their value to God's called community, pastors can influence the church to *provide* community for workers. Pastors do this, for example, through encouraging blue-collar workers to participate in congregational leadership. This may be difficult because, due to a lack of management experience, blue-collar workers might be culturally trained to believe they cannot lead. But this sense of inadequacy provides an opportunity to teach leadership from a biblical perspective.

Meaningful Christian community for blue-collar workers also includes worship typified by believing *and* feeling. Blue-collars are at a disadvantage when ministry revolves around committee meetings where talking is powerful, for their work involves little talk. They value a communal style.[151]

In order to build up the church as a caring community, the pastor will want to model community. Blue-collar people survive by offering help to one another within their community and so will expect a reciprocal kind of relationship with their pastor. For example, if someone with mechanical skills works on the pastor's car, he may expect his pastor to respond by offering premarital counseling to his soon to be married son and future daughter-in-law. Though this might not reconcile well with the prevailing view of pastoral leadership, this is expected in their work world. As a result, the pastor who understands this will, in turn, have a more effective ministry.[152]

---

[149] Sayers, *Creed or Chaos*, 56

[150] Ibid, 57.

[151] Sample, *Blue-Collar Ministry*, 129.

[152] Ibid., 133-137.

For blue-collar workers, reciprocity is an expression of community, not merely a way to earn a living. This attitude cannot be described as a contract; it is more like a covenant.[153] Therefore, effective pastoral ministry to blue-collar workers manifests itself as a web where power and control are negotiated, where the pastor gives and receives. However, reciprocity does not allow one to trade away integrity.

Reciprocity has inherent dangers. Individuals might give the pastor gifts or expensive meals as a means of securing his support for their agendas for the congregation. This can be painful for the unsuspecting and naïve pastor, who believes everyone's motives are honorable. Or, a pastor's ego may be inflated by praise and material gifts that he can never reciprocate. Then, when the pastor will not comply with a church member's view of how to select pastoral staff or choose worship songs, the church member may accuse the pastor of infringing on their friendship. Pastors need to preserve time for themselves and their family so they do not depend on church members to meet all their needs for community. They might also need to graciously decline expensive gifts.

Pastors nurture community for blue-collar Christians through teaching them their vital role in the church. Furthermore, pastoral leadership should shape church life so that it provides community. Finally, they can participate in community with their blue-collar brothers and sisters.

The church equips workers to enhance workplace community

Holy living on the part of Christian workers builds community at work. Although holiness implies separation from the world, one cannot live a holy life in isolation. As Dunham explains, "The Christian is to be distinctly different—set apart by God for God's purpose. The church has often mistaken the meaning of the word 'holiness.' The separation is not *from* the world; it implies expressed difference *in* the world."[154] What does the holy priesthood of 1 Peter 2:5 look like in the workplace? It says, "You also, like living stones, are being built into a spiritual house to be a holy priesthood, offering

[153] Ibid., 139.

[154] Lloyd J. Ogilvie, gen. ed. *The Communicator's Commentary, Old Testament*, 21 vols. (Waco: Word, 1987), vol. 2: *Exodus* by Maxie D. Dunnam, 238.

spiritual sacrifices acceptable to God through Jesus Christ." Dunham continues, "Specifically as priests, we are to speak to the people for God, and we are to speak to God for the people. Our dual vocation is the vocation of witness and prayer."[155] Christian workers bring the *presence* of Christ to work; they demonstrate the *grace* of Christ in relationships; they also do the *work of God* as they use their abilities and disciplines to produce good work; and they heighten *morale* by positive words and attitudes when the atmosphere is often crude and demeaning.

All these aspects of blue-collar, priestly vocation are expressions of love for their fellow workers. According to Luther, "Vocation means that those who are closest at hand, family and fellow-workers, are given by God: it's one's neighbor whom one is to love."[156]

However, instead of encouraging workers as priests in the marketplace, the church often ignores the workplace as the field where Christians serve. This withdrawal by the church coincided, in part, with modern industrial zoning which separated neighborhoods where people live from the zones where they work. Accordingly, congregations built churches in residential neighborhoods, but did not consider how they might influence industrial parks.[157]

But the church is like a lighthouse that does not exist for itself. It is a beacon and a rescue station, not a cruise ship. The church lifts up Christ so that he may draw all people to himself. Therefore, the church is responsible, not only to be the community of Christ for blue-collar workers, but also to equip them to enhance community life in the workplace. They enhance the workplace through priestly ministry and by demonstrating loving, godly service that encourages morale on the job.

---

155 Ibid.

156 Gustaf Wingren, *The Christian's Calling: Luther on Vocation*, trans. C. C. Rasmussen (Edinburgh: Oliver and Boyd, 1957), 172.

157 Holland, *Creative Communion*, 41.

CHAPTER 10

God Calls Workers to Serve with Dignity

The Bible blares out God's call to service. The Apostle Paul wrote, "We pleaded with you, encouraged you, and urged you to live your lives in a way that God would consider worthy. For he called you into his Kingdom to share his glory." (1 Thessalonians 2:12) Paul adds, in Ephesians 4:1, " . . . I, a prisoner for serving the Lord, beg you to lead a life worthy of your calling, for you have been called by God." To clarify the call, believers need to decide whether God's call is a call to general service or a call to a specific career or field.

Does God call workers to general or specific service?

Scripture supports the view that God's call to service is primarily a general calling rather than a call to a specific career. Ryken, however, believes that God calls workers to specific tasks. He argues that, although Scripture often does not use the word "call," God clearly called people like Moses to lead Israel, Bezalel to supervise the construction of the Tabernacle, and Paul to continue as a tentmaker. Ryken says 1 Corinthians 7:17,20 does not teach new Christians to remain Christians but to remain in the occupation or marital situation they were in when converted.[158] Perkins' view was even more prescriptive than Ryken's. He wrote, "A vocation or calling is a certain kind of life, ordained and imposed on man by God for the common good."[159]

---

158 Ryken, *Work and Leisure in Christian Perspective,* 140-142.

159 Perkins, "A Treatise on Vocations," 262.

However, the vast majority of workers cannot remember a moment when God inspired them to take up their work. Consider how the Bible uses the words "call" and "work." For example, 1 Corinthians 7:20-24 translates the word "klesis" as "call".

> Each one should remain in the situation which he was in when God called him. Were you a slave when you were called? Don't let it trouble you—although if you can gain your freedom, do so. For he who was a slave when he was called by the Lord is the Lord's freedman; similarly, he who was a free man when he was called is Christ's slave. You were bought at a price; do not become slaves of men. Brothers, each man, as responsible to God, should remain in the situation God called him to.

When the Apostle Paul wrote the word "klesis," he referred to God's initiative, but this does not imply God calls his people to *specific* roles. Instead, 1 Corinthians 7:17 illustrates God's esteem of all work without declaring one's job to be a life commitment. Furthermore, 1 Corinthians 7:17,20 have been used by some to suggest God's call consists of the place where one serves. Instead, these verses describe the situation a worker is in *when* God calls him or her. The new Christians were not to be concerned about finding God's will through a specific career; they were to rejoice that God's will had found them! Fee writes, " . . . Paul means that by calling a person within a given situation, that situation itself is taken up in the call and thus sanctified by him or her."[160] In other words, God's call does not change one's social status, nor does God force followers of Jesus to change occupations. Moreover, a theological study of work confirms the value of ordinary work roles. " . . . in everyday life that work is judged positively which demonstrates itself to be obedient fulfillment of the divine will, of the law . . . *This applies as much to one's ordinary sphere of work* (cf. Deut. 2:7; 14:29; Job 1:10; Ps. 90[89]:17) as to particular acts of obedience (e.g. Neh. 13:14, a work of love; Ps. 15:2, righteousness; Zeph. 2:3; cf. Ps. 7:4f.; 18:21 ff, italics added)."[161]

---

160 Stevens, "Calling/Vocation," 35.

161 H. C. Hahn, "ergadzomai," in *The New International Dictionary of New Testament Theology*, vol. III, ed. Colin Brown, 1148. (italics mine)

God's calling is not chained to one specific place or role on the planet. Instead, each place or role is a context for expressing God's call to good service. Recognizing the call of God (vocation) is a lifelong journey of celebrations and setbacks through which Christians in the workplace learn to discern God's guiding hand. In other words, workers who serve God learn to identify how his call is being worked out in their lives. Since the Christian worker is no longer at enmity with God, his natural talents are overtaken by the Spirit of God to work for God and to serve other people. The Christian worker should excel in the work he does by giving his best and serving well. Ryken rightly says, "Stated as an ethical principle, any work performed in a moral way for a moral purpose pleases God."[162]

So, the laborer, the truck driver and the waitress may serve the Lord and people with self-respect and dignity. Their self-respect is grounded, not on the esteem others give their jobs, but on God's call to service. Although there might be good reason to change jobs or careers, following Christ does not require workers to move to more morally sanitized workplaces. "Paul's exhortation to 'abide in one's station,' therefore, has genuine relevance for the modern spirit of vocational upheaval. The laborer who makes a commitment to Christ while on a particular job has no reason on that ground to desert his job, if it be respectable, and to cast about at once for something different."[163]

Since the Christian's service on the job pleases God, Christ is walking with the believing blue-collar worker even if she does not recognize that he is present. Similarly, one may not perceive God's call to service because the call is hidden in everyday events such as accidents, circumstances or relationships. John Henry Newman suggested that believers do not have eyes to see the Lord's call and should be more like Jesus' disciple John, who recognized Jesus on the shore after his resurrection (John 21:7). Newman meant that believers should be more aware of Christ's presence and, therefore, his relevance to their circumstances.

Since most workers do not experience a dramatic call to faith, they may not be aware that God's call settled on them at conversion.

---

162 Ryken, *Work and Leisure in Christian Perspective*, 165.

163 Henry, *Aspects of Christian Social Ethics*, 67.

"We ask to know the will of God without guessing that his will is written into our very beings."[164] But workers' lack of awareness does not diminish the reality of their call.

> Laypeople must recognize that they are the vanguard of the church at work in the world, penetrating and perfecting the temporal sphere. For who is the church at work in the world if not mothers, fathers, teachers, government workers, accountants, secretaries, lawyers, artists, doctors, nurses, production workers, and others. Through their unions, businesses, families, agencies, professional associations, community organizations, political parties and other secular institutions, Christians fulfill the church's obligation to sustain and improve the world.[165]

The call to a particular ministry is not taught in the Scriptures as the norm. Instead, through living for Christ at work, blue-collar workers learn to see the call of God on their lives as workers. He integrates his call with their skills, opportunities and even their mistakes.

Renewing perspective; affirming God's call

In order to maintain a godly perspective at work, workers must continually affirm biblical truth. Three truths help workers keep perspective: God values workers; God values their work; and through their work, they bring glory to him.

Because God values workers, the church can counteract the alienation they feel by celebrating various kinds of work. A congregation can set aside Labor Day or other specific Sundays to affirm workers as persons God created and called. God values them regardless of their job status. Thus, the church recognizes all workers, including the unemployed job hunter and the volunteer as persons of worth.[166] Celebrating the intrinsic value of workers contradicts the misconception that the pastor's work is holy while another's work is

---

164 Stevens, "Calling/Vocation," 35.

165 Droel and Pierce, *Confident and Competent*, 23.

166 Peggy Shriver, "Hard Work," in *Christian Century*, May 17/95, 541.

not. Sherman and Hendricks write of this error, " . . . nothing could be further from God's will. The work of God, according to the New Testament, belongs to you, not just your pastor. In a real sense, God has placed part of this world under your management. And like any manager, you must someday give an accounting to the One who hired you. What will He say to you?"[167]

In addition to celebrating various kinds of work, the church should remind Christian blue-collar workers they are better suited for ministry in the workplace than their clergy counterparts. They are familiar with the struggles fellow workers face; they speak the language of the workplace; they understand the issues.

The church must also declare that blue-collar work itself is worthwhile. Scripture declares, "We continually remember before our God and Father *your work produced by faith, your labor prompted by love,* and your endurance inspired by hope in our Lord Jesus Christ." (1 Thessalonians 1:3; italics added) In saying this, the Bible contradicts the perspective that separates spirituality and work. Furthermore, this division does not exist in the Genesis mandate to rule the earth or in other Scriptures like Proverbs 31 where the woman who fears the Lord is also a model worker.[168] So, whether styling hair, bussing tables or carrying lumber, the Christian worker carries out God's acts of love; the work itself is worthwhile.

Spiritual leaders should regularly teach the biblical value of work. Yet, even when the church encourages workers to embrace the dignity of their roles in society, North American culture persistently declares a different value system. A waitress, who parks her old, used car beside her customers' new, luxury models might feel insignificant. Though she has never heard of "The Functional Theory of Stratification," she is living it. The theory states that social inequality is the result of the variety of work required to keep society functioning. In other words, job satisfaction, required skill levels, training, and talent, vary from person to person. As a result, some jobs are more necessary than others for society's survival. Society distributes rewards accordingly and so ends up with different layers of status.[169]

---

167 Sherman and Hendricks, *Your Work Matters to God*, 222.

168 Gordon Preece, "Work," in *The Marketplace Ministry Handbook*, 306.

169 Marvin Yaotsu Chen and Thomas Regan, *Work in the Changing Canadian Society*, (Toronto: Butterworths, 1985), 106.

Blue-collar workers are conscious of these class distinctions. Sample tells of an oil field worker who was bright, well-spoken and easy to work with. However, he appeared insecure and became quiet whenever the boss came on the work site. Sample illustrates this insecurity further by relating a conversation with a worker who felt insignificant because of his position at work. Though he was a skilled cement finisher, he said he could teach others to do his job in one week. "Anybody can do what I'm doing and that's what gives me this feeling," the worker said.[170] He felt like one of society's losers.

North American culture defines winners as those who have the money, the education, the exceptional talent, the looks, or the toys. Often working class people feel like losers in this environment.[171] They do not feel affirmed by the factors that make work rewarding. One study identifies these factors as: Variety, or the degree to which the job requires one to learn different skills or perform different activities; Task identity, or the degree to which the worker is able to complete an entire process: significance—the perceivable impact that one's work has on others, feedback—the amount of information that one receives from significant others about the quality of one's work, autonomy—the amount of control that one is able to exercise over one's work.[172]

Christian workers have another, greater reason to work: the glory of God. God's call is no mere invitation. His call is a command to believe and obey through providing good service for his glory. The cement finisher who feels anybody could learn his job in a week's time could see lasting value in his work if he knew it glorifies God. In other words, work has dignity, not because it is unique or complicated but because it serves the Lord of the universe.

The point is that the Gospel transforms the worker into one called to serve with dignity no matter what the job is. Scripture declares every act prompted by faith to be a worthy act. Paul writes, "With this in mind, we constantly pray for you, that our God may count you worthy of his calling, and that by his power he may fulfill every good purpose of yours *and every act prompted by your faith*." (2 Thessalonians 1:11; italics added)

---

170 Sample, *Blue-Collar Ministry*, 52 53.

171 Ibid., 56, 57.

172 Chen and Regan, *Work in the Changing Canadian Society*, 78,79.

God's call is a call to join him in a life-changing relationship through faith in his Son Jesus Christ. This relationship opens the worker's heart to community with other believers with whom he now shares a common bond through the Holy Spirit. And in this community, the Christian worker is built up to answer the call to serve and glorify God through his work.

PART FOUR

DIMENSIONS OF SERVICE

"If work is to find its right place in the world, it is the duty of the Church to see to it that the work serves God, and that the worker serves the work."[173] Faith in the living God can transform one's experience of work. God calls workers to serve with dignity even in boring, challenging, stressful, or dangerous work. The following pages explore practical implications of obedience to God's call to serve him at work.

173 Sayers, *Creed or Chaos*, 62.

CHAPTER 11

Good Work

Good work is a clearly identifiable theme of Scripture

God's Word emphasizes the value of good work. Examples of competent workers include Joseph, who applied his knowledge in civic administration, Moses, who changed careers from shepherding to leading Israel, and Ruth, who gleaned grain in the field of Boaz. Zacchaeus did not leave his career as a tax collector after Jesus came to his home but paid back fourfold those he had robbed, and he gave half his money to the poor. Also, we know that Luke was a doctor.[174]

If Christians read the Bible as God's letter to workers, they see good work as a means of glorifying the Father in heaven (Matthew 5:16). Consequently, good work serves the world in God's name. When Christian workers contribute to the good of the workplace, others may ask what motivates them (1 Peter 2:12). Furthermore, Scripture urges workers to serve well even when the workplace is hostile to faith. For example, Jeremiah told Jewish captives in Babylon to settle down and work for the prosperity and peace of the city (Jeremiah 29:4-7).

Thus, Scripture affirms the value of doing good work. Through clear directives and vivid examples, the Bible encourages God's people to do their work well for the glory of God.

---

174 Jacobsen, *Hearts to God, Hands to Work*, 31,32.

Good work is a natural result of knowing God

Knowing God ought to motivate one to perform work well. But seeing one's work as a place to honor the Lord is especially difficult for workers with supervisors who treat employees like tools to be used, broken, and replaced. For example, an oil company employee complained that no matter how much she does, she cannot please her boss.[175] When the job environment hurts morale, Christian workers need courage derived from knowing they are God's called people.

Laborers can derive courage from knowing they are created in God's image. As such, they are stewards of creation, which God pronounced "good." Christ, in his resurrection body, the body of a carpenter, appeared to and ate with his disciples. By doing so, he gave evidence that God values his creation and works to redeem it.[176] Knowing that *God* values good work as part of his created order encourages workers when workplace morale is low.

Furthermore, God's love for his creation helps workers discern what kind of work they should do. Some jobs are inadequate as expressions of God's creativity no matter how hard one works. "For instance, is the best use of your life the creation or merchandising of so much of the kitsch sold in roadside shops—tumblers that say, 'I'm a Pisces'; furry dice to hang from rear-view mirrors; bumper stickers that advertise one's sexual libido?"[177] Perhaps the solution to this puzzling question is found in the worker's motive for work. Can he put his heart into it, because he knows that God cares about the level of his effort?

Christian workers also produce good work because they know that God *called* them to serve. As noted previously, variations of the Greek work "kalein" (to call) appear almost 200 times in the New Testament. In each of these uses, God calls people to salvation that includes service.[178] For example, a laborer who was injured on the job was retained, not because the boss had compassion, but because the worker did good work as a result of his Christian values.

---

[175] Conversation with a front office worker, 2007.

[176] Ronald J. Sider, *One-Sided Christianity*, (Grand Rapids: Zondervan, 1993), 92.

[177] Sherman, *Keeping Your Head Up*, 85.

[178] Barnette, *Christian Calling and Vocation*, 16,17.

Good work is not an effort to *find* fellowship with God. Rather, it *expresses* God's calling to a relationship with himself. Through faith in Christ, believing workers are already part of Christ's church; their works are not an effort to enter the church. Instead, their vocation is service to other members of the community. Luther interpreted vocation, as in 1 Corinthians 7:20, as a contribution to community.

> What a fine condition it would be if it so happened that everyone looked after his own responsibilities, and yet thereby served his neighbor, so that together they traveled on the right road to heaven . . . Everyone ought to look after his own work, and not that of another; so we should live together in simple obedience, in a harmony of many missions and manifold works.[179]

Workers who know they are called by God have the advantage of knowing they work for Christ. They believe they can trust him during cutbacks or layoffs. Instead of being ruined by anxiety during times of stress, they can remain focused because Christ is their provider.[180] As a result, they produce good work with confidence in the following precepts of God's word.

- "Whatever your hand finds to do, do it with all your might." (Ecclesiastes 9:10)
- "Whatever you do, work at it with all your heart, as working for the Lord, not for men . . ." (Colossians 3:23)
- "All who are under the yoke of slavery should consider their masters worthy of full respect, so that God's name and our teaching may not be slandered." (1Timothy 6:1)

Therefore, a personal relationship with the living God motivates quality work because God created workers to be stewards of his good creation.

---

179 Wingren, *The Christian's Calling*, 178, 179.

180 Sherman, *Keeping Your Head Up*, 196, 197.

Good work is a competent witness

The first responsibility of a Christian worker is good work.[181] The church should not only teach workers to stop getting drunk and attend church on Sunday; the church should also teach workers to do good work. In fact, Sayers makes the point that the piety associated with church attendance is useless if the worker's poor craftsmanship insults God.[182] Diehl writes, "Competence is our basic level of ministry. Tradition has it that St. Augustine was criticized by his Christian friends because he bought his sandals from a non-Christian craftsman when there was a Christian sandal maker in the same town. He defended his actions by explaining that he did too much walking to buy inferior sandals."[183]

The frequency of sloppy work would be severely curbed if workers would stick to the work they do best.[184] "Our greatest witness to our faith in our place of work is our degree of competency. Unless we are competent, our witness as Christians is not seriously received by this world."[185]

Competent blue-collar workers have a vital ministry in the world of work. Paul Stevens tells the story of Nicu Toader, a mechanic during the cruel communist days of Romania. He was also an active leader of a large underground church. When he was summoned by the local Chief Justice of the Secret Police in the city of Timisoara, Nicu feared his freedom, and possibly his life, was over. Moreover, he feared pressure to cooperate with the Secret Police. He imagined the "interview" would consist of sinister threats against his young daughter and son if he did not provide police with information about other believers. Instead, the police chief sent Nicu to the chief's home to fix his home appliances. As he handed Nicu the keys to his apartment, he said he knew that Nicu was a serious Repenter (the term used for an evangelical Christian). As a result, he trusted that Nicu would neither steal his food or valuables, nor look through his personal papers. "And," the chief continued, "I also know that you are

---

181 Henry, *Aspects of Christian Social Ethics*, 70.

182 Colson and Eckerd, *Why America Doesn't Work*, 94.

183 Diehl, *The Monday Connection*, 30.

184 Ryken, *Work and Leisure in Christian Perspective*, 148.

185 Diehl, *The Monday Connection*, 41.

absolutely the best mechanic in the entire City of Timisoara. When you fix things they stay fixed! Your silly faith and your work skills bring you to my office this afternoon."[186] Stevens continues,

> This was the first of several calls for personal help by the secret police of Communist Timisoara. After the Christmas 1989 Revolution in Romania, the Chief admitted that his Bucaresti superiors had told him to arrest the leaders and crush the underground church in Timisoara. When Nicu's name appeared on the arrest list, the order was permanently deferred by the Chief. It appears that God protected his church by the work excellence and public reputation of a skilled mechanic whose personal character convinced the chief to keep him around."[187]

Good work meets human need

One purpose of good work is to meet human need. Proverbs affirms this, saying, "He who works his land will have abundant food, but the one who chases fantasies will have his fill of poverty." (Proverbs 28:19) "The laborer's appetite works for him; his hunger drives him on." (Proverbs 16:26) "A sluggard does not plow in season; so at harvest time he looks but finds nothing." (Proverbs 20:4) In other words, work serves the essential purpose of providing for legitimate needs. Paul censured Christians who were not willing to work: "We hear that some among you are idle. They are not busy; they are busybodies. Such people we command and urge in the Lord Jesus Christ to settle down and earn the bread they eat." (2 Thessalonians 3:11,12) Paul was writing to new Christians, telling them that their new faith contrasted with their culture's Greek philosophy that valued leisure and deplored work.

Jesus illustrated the value of work as a means of meeting human need. As a tradesman, he was immersed in the precursor to blue-collar culture (Mark 6:3), and he had been raised by his "blue-collar" step-father Joseph (Matthew 13:55). Moreover, Jesus chose disciples who were fishermen and tax collectors, not rulers.

---

186 Stevens, *Doing God's Business*, 54,55. (Stevens credits Alec Woodhull for this story)

187 Ibid., 55.

Good work meets a variety of human needs, both material and emotional. Sayers writes, "We should ask of an enterprise, not 'will it pay?' but 'is it good?'; of a man, not 'what does he make?' but 'what is his work worth?'; of goods, not 'can we induce people to buy them?' but 'are they useful things well made?'; of employment, not 'how much a week?' but 'will it exercise my faculties to the utmost?'"[188]

Yet, the Bible does not say workers should not enjoy material prosperity that might result from good work.[189] Ecclesiastes 5:18,19 says,

> Then I realized that it is good and proper for a man to eat and drink, and to find satisfaction in his toilsome labor under the sun during the few days of life God has given him—for this is his lot. Moreover, when God gives any man wealth and possessions, and enables him to enjoy them, to accept his lot and be happy in his work—this is a gift of God.

Furthermore, Joseph and Daniel were both materially successful, and the Apostle Paul participated in a successful business as a tentmaker.

Meeting human needs is a legitimate purpose of good work. Those who work for God's glory can choose to find satisfaction in meeting a wide variety of needs through their work. And they enjoy the good results of their labor, including material well-being.

Good work is satisfying when done by faith

Ultimately, work is not fully satisfying unless it is accompanied by faith in the living God, the Creator and Redeemer of both work and workers. Blue-collar workers who dedicate their work to God can see their jobs as fields in which to express their God-given dignity. Otherwise, they might measure their worth by social status or compare themselves with white-collar workers. Will they view their work as good work for God or will they see it as unimportant drudgery?

---

188 Sayers, *Doing God's Business*, 52.

189 Ryken, *Work and Leisure in Christian Perspective*, 167.

Developing a Christian perspective on work is difficult. A prevailing attitude in today's workforce is that blue-collar work is *not* satisfying. Kohn and Schooler, in a study of blue-collar men, found that

> . . . blue-collar men were in work roles that require conformity to external authority . . . Men of higher social class valued intrinsically satisfying work, and blue-collar men attached more importance to extrinsic factors, such as "pay, fringe benefits, the supervisor, co-workers, the hours of work, how tiring the work is, job security, and not being under too much pressure."[190]

But is faith in God enough to make work satisfying? If workers want to please God, are they doing enough by doing good work, or is God only satisfied if they continually find opportunities to tell co-workers about their faith, set an example of godly speech, or help settle disputes between colleagues? No, workers can be assured that God accepts good work as an act of praise. Scripture refers to the Christian's body as an offering acceptable to God (Romans 12:1). Furthermore, while in this body, believers do good work by faith, not because they can see their reward. And, while in the body, they make it their goal to please God, knowing he will give them what they are due for their work (2 Corinthians 5:7-10).

Therefore, by faith one can install new windshields in vehicles with the knowledge that this good work pleases God. This work can be satisfying, not only because new, clearer windshields promote safer driving, but also because the act of installation is an act of service, by faith, to the Lord.

If extrinsic factors are not satisfying, and if workers believe their work is of little value, they may neglect workmanship. Kaiser writes, "Work done without zest or spirit or indolently is often thinly disguised injustice. The dull and listless teacher, the repetitious and rambling preacher, the slovenly housekeeper, the workman who dawdles at his task—all come dangerously close to doing useless work."[191] But when

---

190 Sample, *Blue-Collar Ministry*, 48,49.

191 Kaiser, *Theology of Work*, 11.

Christian workers believe their work matters to God, they devote themselves to doing their jobs well.

When workers don't believe their work is important, they may assign value to being "top dog"—achieving power—instead of serving God at work. Tex Sample tells of an oilfield foreman who described his work as a place where being "number one" was the ultimate value: "I don't want to change it, I want to take advantage of it. Someday, I want to be at the top." But after retiring and living better than most working-class people, he felt he had never made it to the top.[192]

The desire to be on top of the work pyramid betrays selfishness not unlike the belief that slavery is acceptable. This belief implies that status and material gain have value, while people are mere tools in the service of materialism. "Slavery, by placing the material above the spiritual, the fruits of labor above the rights of the worker, subordinated man himself to material gain. It placed human beings in the service of greed and every debasing passion. Moral ideals were not permitted to stand in the way of material gain."[193]

These moral ideals contradict the notion that wealth and status assign value to people. If workers adopt this notion, they focus on getting free of work rather than working for God's glory. Ignatius of Antioch, writing to Polycarp of Smyrna, stated that one should not treat slaves with an air of superiority. Neither, he insisted, should slaves be haughty but, " . . . for the glory of God they should render all the better service so as to obtain a better freedom from God. They should not pine for release at the expense of the community; otherwise, they turn out to be slaves of unruly appetites."[194] "Slaves of unruly appetites"—what an apt description for *my* generation. We might be the most free people in history, free to live as we please, yet in bondage to the belief that status is more satisfying than service. By contrast, Christian workers believe that faith, hope and love, not status, give lasting value to work (1Cor. 3:10-15; 13:13). Work done in this way will last, purified by fire, in the new heaven and the new earth (2 Peter 3:12-13). Truly, work has an aspect of lasting satisfaction.

Faith in the living God transforms work for blue-collar workers. Good work is clearly identifiable as a priority in Scripture. In fact,

---

192 Sample, *Blue-Collar Ministry*, 31.

193 Kaiser, *Theology of Work*, 24.

194 194 Ibid., 20.

good work is the fruit of knowing God, and provides a competent witness to co-workers. Besides being a clear witness, work meets human need. Ultimately all work, except that which contradicts God's word, can be seen as an act of faithful service to God.

CHAPTER 12

Pay and Its Problems

Receiving pay is a legitimate motive for work, although the quantity of pay is a provision rather than a right. On the scale of workplace priorities, however, pay is not the most important element of work. In fact, workers want to be treated with dignity more than they want high wages.[195]

Money is a legitimate motive for work

Earning money in order to support oneself and one's household is a godly activity. Through working, Christians avoid becoming social parasites.[196] The following Scriptures emphasize this.

> In the name of the Lord Jesus Christ, we command you, brothers, to keep away from every brother who is idle and does not live according to the teaching you received from us. For you yourselves know how you ought to follow our example. We were not idle when we were with you, nor did we eat anyone's food without paying for it. On the contrary, we worked night and day, laboring and toiling so that we would not be a burden to any of you. We did this, not because we do not have the right to such help, but in order

---

195 Kenneth H Blanchard, "Motivational Factors Test For Managers," quoted in Pine Tree Management Skills Inc., *Management Skills For Front Line Managers*, (seminar taught in Edmonton, Alberta), Module 1

196 Ryken, *Work and Leisure in Christian Perspective*, 168.

> to make ourselves a model for you to follow. For even when we were with you, we gave you this rule: "If a man will not work, he shall not eat." We hear that some among you are idle. They are not busy; they are busybodies. Such people we command and urge in the Lord Jesus Christ to settle down and earn the bread they eat. (2 Thessalonians 3:6-12)
>
> Surely you remember, brothers, our toil and hardship; we worked night and day in order not to be a burden to anyone while we preached the gospel of God to you. (1 Thessalonians 2:9)

Building on Scriptures like these, the church ought to preach a message of individual responsibility rather than a health and wealth gospel. "'If a man will not work, let him not eat' were not compassionless words; they were a call to individual responsibility."[197] Being well paid does not defile one's work. Some Christians, who feel uneasy about money as a good motive for working, prefer to see the workplace only as a field for evangelism.[198] However, the Bible values work as a means of caring for creation and providing for physical needs. Scripture does not reveal a cavalier disregard for physical matter.[199]

Blue-collar workers understand the necessity of work for pay. Hobart Foote, a utility man, said "I feed the family and with two teen-aged kids, there's a lot of wants. And we're payin' for two cars. And I have brought home a forty-hour paycheck for Lord knows how long. And that's why I work."[200]

Furthermore, choosing a job according to its pay scale is legitimate for Christian workers. Richard Baxter believed a Christian worker should take a better paying opportunity as long as the higher functions of work, such as the public good and care of one's own soul, were in place.[201]

No matter what other importance we add to work, it remains a means of income. Moreover, wages should be just as Pope Jean Paul

---

197 Colson and Eckerd, *Why America Doesn't Work*, 96.

198 Sherman and Hendricks, *Your Work Matters To God*, 182.

199 Kaiser, *Theology of Work*, 59.

200 Terkel, *Working*, 235.

201 Richard Baxter, "Direction About Our Labor And Callings," in *Callings*, 284.

II emphasized: " . . . wages, that is to say remuneration for work, are still a practical means whereby the vast majority of people can have access to those goods which are intended for common use: both the goods of nature and manufactured goods."[202] Work and pay are so closely associated in western culture that most people think of work in terms of paid employment.[203]

This cultural focus on pay magnifies tension between workers and management. By contrast, Scripture commands Christian employers to pay their workers fairly. James wrote,

> Now listen, you rich people, weep and wail because of the misery that is coming upon you. Your wealth has rotted, and moths have eaten your clothes. Your gold and silver are corroded. Their corrosion will testify against you and eat your flesh like fire. You have hoarded wealth in the last days. Look! The wages you failed to pay the workmen who mowed your fields are crying out against you. The cries of the harvesters have reached the ears of the Lord Almighty (James 5:1-4).

This call to fair remuneration is no less relevant today than when God inspired James with these words.

Through working for pay, blue-collar workers participate in God-ordained service and they avoid becoming a burden to society. However, they are not usually paid as well as their white-collar counterparts. In some cases, they are not paid fairly at all. How then should blue-collar workers react to this reality?

Pay is God's provision, rather than merely a human right

Christian workers have a higher, more enduring goal than earning money. The chief motive underlying the Christian's work is that God will say "Well done" to all who serve him faithfully regardless of their income or job status. Yet, Christians in the workforce may easily become caught up in the quest for wealth, especially when

---

202 Pope Jean Paul II, *Laborem Exercens*, quoted in Stanley Hauerwas, "Work as Co-Creation," 52.

203 Chen and Regan, *Work in the Changing Canadian Society*, 5.

commodity prices are high and companies pay very well. However, in the parable of the talents, Jesus affirmed faithful service rather than equal distribution of wealth (Matthew 25:14-30). Moreover, the Apostle Paul professed to know the secret of serving the Lord in either plenty or want; the secret was that God's love and purpose were not conditioned by economics.[204]

The ultimate *reward*—affirmation for good stewardship of one's life—is also the ultimate *motive* for work. Christian workers work from a position of security. Specifically, they are secure in the covenant they have with God. "The totality of the covenant means that one has already been 'spoken for' and is no longer available to become the slave of another master."[205] While the world has a contractual view of work, Christ's followers have a covenant view: they work out of love for God and he provides for them. In this way, work is the workers' part in fulfilling God's creation covenant.

So, Christian workers have a deeper motive and a higher goal than being paid. What other motives balance workers' need for remuneration?

Where pay fits on the scale of priorities

Culture values accumulation of wealth, but Jesus said a man's life does not consist of the amount of things he owns (Luke 12:15). Work and the things it affords are not enough to fill workers' hearts. However, factory workers and assembly line workers often value the size of their incomes and the non-work lifestyle they can afford as the chief benefits of their jobs.[206]

Although blue-collar workers often measure their success in terms of income, they want their work to mean more. " . . . 79% of the workers who are paid based on performance are happy with their pay, compared with 60% of those whose pay is not based on performance . . . 'People want to be rewarded for what they put into a job . . . they want to have a positive return on their investment of their time and effort . . . '"[207]

---

204 Shriver, "Hard Work," 541.

205 Haughey, *Converting Nine to Five*, 26.

206 Chen and Regan, *Work in the Changing Canadian Society*, 79.

207 "Executive Pay Too High, Workers Say," *National Post*, 27 June, 2007, WK 7.

In contrast to the world's consumerism and want, Christians are to be contented when their needs are met. John the Baptist cautioned, "be content with your wages," (Luke 3:14), and Jesus said, "The worker is worthy of his hire." (Luke 10:7)[208] While the Bible does not supply a paradigm for income distribution, one could argue in favor of income that is sufficient for living, while cautioning against unlimited accumulation of wealth.[209]

Workers want more than money

Who can blame factory workers for being concerned with their income and job security? Workers want to be treated with dignity rather than used as instruments of the company. Charles Colson illustrates the results of treating workers with dignity. Ellis was a window washer who worked slowly and complained too much. Mr. Wessner, his boss, listened to Ellis describe a work related injury that caused searing pain whenever he gripped the squeegee too tightly. Wessner asked Ellis if he liked window washing and he replied that he really didn't but it was the only job he could find. So, Wessner offered Ellis a job as a floor finisher, a job that would not strain his arm, and he became the best floor finisher and quickest learner on staff.[210] Ellis is an example of a wage earner who found dignity on the job. He is not alone in this search. "Younger workers aren't giving in to the idea that they don't make a difference. Aging baby boomers are back to exploring their souls. More and more of us are on a quest for greater meaning in our lives."[211]

Employees at Cummins Engine developed the following list of core values with which they could measure their own performance. Notice that the list focuses on people.

- trust, respect, and equity for workers
- a commitment to the worker's full potential
- training as a keystone for attaining organizational excellence

---

208 Henry, *Aspects of Christian Social Ethics*, 66.

209 Peter Nijkamp, "Socioethical Aspects of Labour," in *Labour of Love*, ed. Josina Van Nuis Zylstra, (Toronto: Wedge Publishing, 1980), 60.

210 Colson and Eckerd, *Why America Doesn't Work*, 158,159.

211 James M Kouzes and Barry Z. Posner, *The Leadership Challenge*, 3rd ed., (San Francisco: Jossey-Bass, 2002), xxii.

- the worker's participation in decision making [212]

This kind of movement toward dignity in the workplace illustrates the God-implanted desire workers have to be regarded as valuable. This implicit longing finds its true fulfillment in service to the living God whether the service is for paid work or not. Alan Richardson, in a discussion of the meaning of the New Testament Greek word "doulos"—translated "servant" or "slave"—writes, "'Worker' is perhaps the best modern rendering of 'doulos,' even though it does not carry with it the suggestion of being tied to someone's occupation and to one's employer."[213] Thus, in the New Testament, master and worker could have a relationship of mutual respect (Colossians 3:22-4:1; 1 Timothy 6:2). Scripture places high value on the relationship between boss and worker, albeit in the context of the family of believers. Therefore, the church should be concerned about work that forces people into degrading or harmful situations.[214] Pope John Paul II wrote,

> But the church considers it her task always to call attention to the dignity and rights of those who work, to condemn situations in which that dignity and those rights are violated, and to help to guide the above-mentioned changes so as to ensure authentic progress by man and society.[215]

Can labor unions also retain a significant role in ensuring dignity as well as fair pay for their members? The former Roman Catholic Pope thought so, but questioned their effectiveness because of their political ties.

> Unions do not have the character of political parties struggling for power; they should not be subjected to the decision of political parties or have too close links with them. In fact, in such a situation they easily lose contact with their specific role, which is to secure the just rights of workers within the framework of the common good of the

212 Colson and Eckerd, *Why America Doesn't Work*, 125.
213 Richardson, *The Biblical Doctrine of Work*, 39.
214 Sayers, *Creed or Chaos*, 56.
215 Pope Jean Paul II, *Laborem Exercens*, 4.

> whole of society; instead they become an instrument used for other purposes.[216]

Moreover, the adversarial approach of most labor-management negotiations hampers resolution and destroys trust. The adversarial system fails to treat workers as responsible people. Instead, this system focuses on raising wages and reducing work hours.[217]

Does the union offer meaningful support to the Christian, blue-collar worker? To a limited degree it does; however, unions tend to focus solely on issues of pay and benefits rather than the Christian value of service to God and mankind.[218] As one studies the Bible's message about workers and their need for support, one questions a traditional posture of some conservative Christians—that unions are, generally speaking, the enemy. Moreover, the dignity given workers in the Bible would move one to call on unions and management to show faith in each other instead of posturing for power. Workers often get lost in the shuffle between unions and management. Union members are sometimes afraid to contradict their unions for fear of suffering reprisals, rejection and perhaps violence.

Christian workers have a biblical foundation for dignified service and the church of Jesus Christ should be vocal about abuses to workers. Workers want fair treatment from managers. They want to be paid fairly and valued as persons. Unions could play a stronger role in solving the problems of the workplace if they broadened their concerns to include issues of human dignity more often than merely fighting for higher wages.

Still, earning money is a legitimate motive for working and it is reasonable for workers to expect fair pay. But income is ultimately part of God's provision. Therefore, Christian workers have a deeper motive for work than money; they work to serve the living God. And while pay continues to be an important objective, workers want meaningful jobs in which fair pay is accompanied by fair treatment. The church should have a voice in the community,

---

216 Ibid., 47.

217 Harry Antonides, "From Confrontation to Partnership," in *Labour of Love*, ed. Van Nuis Zylstra, 111.

218 Grootenboer, *About Work and Unions*, 16.

calling business and unions to work for the benefit of the workers rather than their own power structures. Workers want and need to be treated with dignity.

CHAPTER 13

Relationships at Work

Since God calls blue-collar workers to relationships, how do workers integrate relationships and work? In other terms, what does love look like on the job? Relationships among workers influence the quality of their service. Furthermore, workers who participate in small support groups in their churches can encourage each other to contribute to healthy relationships at work.

Relationships and the value of persons in the workplace

God intended the first people, Adam and Eve, to live in satisfying, productive community. The Genesis creation account is, in part, a story about the relationship between two people on the job. Paul Stevens writes, "Males are not the image of God and neither are females. We are designed for community, to experience, to build it, and to extend it by being fruitful, multiplying, and filling the earth." [219]

However, the relationship Adam and Eve enjoyed deteriorated when they sinned. As a result, their intimacy and communication were overshadowed by a drive to dominate each other. The first couple's loss of communion now infiltrates the fabric of every relationship. Holland writes, "As Genesis then tells us, this violence in the most intimate and personal process of sexuality constantly works its way outward to wider ecological-social-spiritual alienation."[220]

---

219 Stevens, *Doing God's Business*, 27.

220 Holland, *Creative Communion*, 51.

Alienation corrupts the workplace in very practical ways. For example, a boss tells one of the drivers in his trucking firm to treat his swampers (the men who help off-load heavy cargo) roughly or they will not get enough work done. The swampers, he explains, are "scrubs" he had to hire because of a shortage of good workers. The driver, a Christian, observes how another driver goes as far as injuring swampers so that they will quit their jobs. On top of the pressure to get productivity from people who lack motivation, the driver deals with aggressive people at job sites. Describing these pressures, he says, "It messes with your head when it's steady. I keep my head down or I have conflict."[221]

The boss sees the problem of lost productivity, but he cannot see the root problem or the solution. Even in scenarios like this, God can empower workers to seek balance between their own needs and the needs of others. Jesus did not lay down a strict method of loving others. Instead, he told us to love as he loves (John 13:34). Such self-giving love counters the world's pattern of serving self first. When Jesus commanded his disciples to love their enemies, he explained, "If you love those who love you, what reward will you get? Are not even tax collectors doing that?" (Matthew 5:47) Again, this love stands out like white paint on a dark canvass. The worker who loves others cares about their needs with the same care he gives his own needs (Matthew 22:39).

The love Jesus commands is not sentimental, nor are blue-collar workers often inclined to engage in sentimentality. Instead, Jesus' love often appears at work as quiet endurance and service to others. Another example of quiet love that attracts attention involves a young laborer who endured abuse and ridicule from a bully who frequently threatened him. When the bully was about to move to another workplace, he approached the laborer and apologized for his behavior. He said he was glad to know him and that if there were ten men like him in this particular shop, it would be a great place to work.[222]

Love has been hampered at work since the first workers sinned. Although workplace tensions and culture raise obstacles to loving others, Christian workers have the challenging job of loving their co-

---

221 Conversation with a driver, 2007.

222 Conversation with a laborer, 2009.

workers. Simple respect and concern for others at work helps create an atmosphere where others sense the love of God.

Relationships motivate work

Love motivates service at work. The worker's current job is usually an important place of service, in part because he has many relationships there. Moreover, service improves when one is content with one's workplace.

Loving others is the habitat in which one works responsibly (1 Thessalonians 4:9-12). Luther urged his parishioners not to abandon their occupations in order to live in a monastery. Instead, he said they should " . . . conscientiously serve their neighbor within the stations that God had placed them."[223]

Work teams illustrate the motivating power of relationships. They contribute to excellence in manufacturing because, as team members care for excellent work, they learn to care for each other. "It comes down to a homely truth: in addition to income, humans find work rewarding because their companions at work show some love for them, treat them as valuable and work with them with a measure of mutual esteem to produce something deemed valuable to others."[224]

Loving relationships at work motivate contentment with the work. Subsequently, contented workers give their best, because of their commitment to excellence.

Relationships and the power of the group

Individualism hampers relationships in North American blue-collar culture. However, churches that nurture regularly scheduled small groups encourage Christians to overcome individualism by becoming transparent with each other.

Christ's followers are not the only people seeking meaningful relationships at work. As a case in point, Kouzes and Posner write that social capital has overtaken intellectual capital as the most important value in the workplace. They define social capital as " . . . the collective

---

223 Lee Hardy, *The Fabric of This World*, (Grand Rapids: Eerdmans, 1990), 47.

224 Donald W. Shriver Jr., "Vocation and Work in an Era of Downsizing," in *Christian Century*, May 17/95, 539.

value of people who know each other and what they'll do for each other."[225] Since social capital is so important, Kouzes and Posner raise the questions, "How do you build a workplace where people can trust each other and trust the institution? . . . How can leaders deliver on the promise of offering exciting and meaningful work and treating even the most temporary of workers with dignity and respect?"[226] Placing value on relationships at work contradicts the common self-centered ethic that first asks, "What's in it for me?"[227]

Christian workers learn to serve better by meeting with a group of believers who are competent in similar work. Such a group provides advice and an opportunity to share experiences.[228] One feature of a group like this is its commitment to meet regularly. Another feature is confidentiality. Ultimately, the group's goal is to help participants live out their faith.[229] Groups such as this are practical expressions of the priesthood of believers who worship together and encourage one another in faithful service. Some business groups, for example, have promoted meaningful dialogue and learning among Christians who have similar workplace roles.[230]

The church can respond to the emergence of social capital by reaffirming God's call to community and helping believers develop supportive relationships. Small groups of like-minded people with similar workplace roles are a key method of building this support.

Nurturing healthier workplace relationships

Christians, who are encouraged through relationships with other like-minded believers, nurture healthy relationships at work. They do so in various ways, including their commitment to excellent work as part of the workplace team, setting an example, asking oneself what Jesus would do in a given situation, refusing to gossip and offering compassion.

---

225 Kouzes and Posner, *The Leadership Challenge*, xx.

226 Ibid., xxii.

227 Ryken, *Work and Leisure in Christian Perspective*, 172.

228 Diehl, *The Monday Connection*, 48.

229 Ibid., 51.

230 Corpath Groups have been ministries of Christian Business Ministries Canada.

Peter Ochs' real estate development company was driven by the belief that God values people, therefore, Peter wanted to value people too. As a result, the company formed these basic values:

- Excellence in everything we do
- An environment of teamwork and trust
- Value of the individual employee
- Commitment to our home buyers
- Executing details well
- Integrity in the conduct of our business[231]

A commitment to excellence is important because God values people, and therefore he values what they do. The end result is that excellence enriches workplace relationships and morale.

One can never underestimate the power of a good example at work. Christians influence the relationships around them as light infiltrates darkness. For example, the colleagues of a Christian worker suffering from a migraine, told her to "get it together because *you* affect everyone else."[232] A young worker named Tom was impressed when D.J. DePree, the chairman of Herman Miller, came to talk with him not long after Tom began working for the company. Another employee told him that DePree would often be found listening to workers and getting their ideas. If an idea could not be implemented, he would inform employees of the reason. Thirteen years later, Tom credits D.J. DePree and his sons for their influence, through their honest lifestyles, on Tom's spiritual values. Furthermore, he believes the participatory management style has been critical to his work success.[233]

The question, "What would Jesus do?" has been criticized by some Christians because it does not address the critical difference between Jesus' divine nature and workers' human nature. However, when a manager, co-worker, or client is screaming at a laborer, "What would Jesus do?" is likely the best choice of all the phrases going through the mind of the one being yelled at. For instance, when the neighbor's bull tore down the fence around a Christian farmer's property, the neighbor screamed at him, blaming him for having his heifers too

---

231 Colson and Eckert, *Why America Doesn't Work*, 129.

232 Conversation with a Christian laboratory technician, 2005.

233 Ibid., 143.

near the fence. The Christian neighbor quietly helped the neighbor round up the bull. He then promised to round up his heifers and go home. He later confided that the question, "What would Jesus do?" helped him deal with his attitude in the heat of the moment. Considering the character of Jesus focused his attention away from the conflict and on to serving the Lord and his angry neighbor.[234]

Angry neighbors are difficult, but what should a Christian worker do if her supervisor is acting in an unjust manner? Since gossip is such a common practice in the workplace, she might first of all refuse to talk about the manager behind his back. She might also offer objective suggestions to co-workers about how to approach the situation, using legitimate means at their disposal. Steve Jacobsen tells of someone in his congregation

> . . . whose hospital lab had been permeated by a gossipy, complaining atmosphere. This [parishioner] told how she decided one day she would simply refuse to go along with conversations that were critical of co-workers, not by making a great speech but by simply redirecting the conversation. People at first were surprised that she wasn't joining in, but eventually the negative atmosphere dissipated. A simple, quiet act had tangible results.[235]

Caring about others is powerful, as Maxine Dennis, a grocery store cashier, illustrates. Dennis believes that she does God's work by doing her work well. Specifically, she tries to make customers feel special by showing compassion. Noting that an elderly, lonely looking man was purchasing a box of birdseed, she said, "Oh, I see you have a pet bird too. Aren't they fun?" The man's face brightened as he told her about his parakeet. He referred to the bird affectionately as something that had been good company since his wife had died six months before. Maxine shares the conversation:

> "It must be difficult to cope with the loss of a loved one," I commented thoughtfully as I placed his bundles into his

---

[234] Conversation with a Christian farmer, 2006.

[235] Jacobsen, *Hearts to God, Hands to Work*, 39.

> shopping cart. "It certainly is," he sighed heavily. "We were married for 50 years, my Mary and me," he added, his eyes twinkling brightly from her memory. "How wonderful. Please come back and visit with me soon. I really enjoyed talking with you today," I told him as he started to leave. "You bet," he answered. I noticed that although the loneliness on his face was still there, it had diminished somewhat . . . I had taken a few minutes to care and listen to a fellow human being, succeeding in making at least a tiny difference in this one, precious life . . . Observation and perception are the two tools I use most often to do God's work while doing mine.[236]

Christians ought to be equipped and encouraged to pass relational health on to their workplaces. Through commitment to excellence, mentoring, asking how Jesus might deal with conflict situations, refusing to gossip, and offering compassion, they nurture healthier workplace relationships.

---

[236] Maxine Dennis, "Compassion is the Most Vital Tool of My Trade," in *Of Human Hands*, ed. Pierce, 49-51.

CHAPTER 14

Verbal Witness

Christians value telling others of God's gift of hope through Jesus. Blue-collar Christians embrace this mandate no less than other believers do. But lack of clarity about verbal witness leads Christians to commit harmful errors when they attempt to share their faith. And even with a clear understanding of one's faith, talking about it can be difficult. Workplace witnesses need effective methods of communicating faith, and, instead of forcing conversations about spiritual matters, they need to wait for God to provide opportunities.

The mandate of verbal witness

Jesus commanded his followers to tell others about him.

> All authority in heaven and on earth has been given to me. Therefore go and make disciples of all nations, baptizing them in the name of the Father and of the Son and of the Holy Spirit, and teaching them to obey everything I have commanded you. And surely I am with you always, to the very end of the age. (Matthew 28:18-20)

Scripture describes witnesses as God's fellow workers; some plant the good news, some nurture it, and God makes it grow (1 Corinthians 3:6-9). No matter what sort of work Christians do, one element of their work is witness. " . . . the proper work of Christians is the furtherance of the Gospel and the service of the purpose of God."[237]

The relationship of verbal witness to work

Some Christians in the marketplace perceive work as little more than a context for sharing their faith. The following illustrates this emphasis.

> Sometimes we mistakenly say, "They work so that they can proclaim Christ." It would be more correct to say, "They work as they proclaim Christ." Early believers used their jobs and their homes as platforms to proclaim the gospel. We need to do the same. Have we lost the simplicity of their method?[238]

A deep, wide canyon separates holistic integration of faith at work and some perceptions of witness. One might envision attempts to cross this gap in the following ways. The "dare devil" approach: Like a motorcycle-riding stunt man, willing to risk jumping the canyon, the workplace dare devil is willing to charge across the divide between church and work culture. She hopes to "land" safely enough at work each day to show co-workers what a difference Christ makes in her life. Her basic belief is that she has nothing in common with "those people" at work. Instead, her real life is back across the canyon at church. Work is valuable only as a temporary landing area where she might show people how badly they need Jesus.

The "emergency drop" approach: Just as search and rescue aircraft drop supplies to victims of tidal waves or hurricanes, the "emergency drop" Christian parachutes in books, CDs, DVDs and Bible study materials in hopes that someone will find and use them in the workplace. His basic belief is that he is behind enemy lines and his ammunition is the material he hopes to get people to read, hear or watch. Work is an instrument for distribution.

---

237 Richardson, *The Biblical Doctrine of Work*, 31.

238 Kent Humphreys, *Lasting Investments*, (Colorado Springs: Navpress, 2004), 102.

The "send missionaries" approach: Importing techniques from mass evangelism combined with overseas missionary enterprise, this approach acknowledges the necessity of the gospel. Yet, it is motivated by the belief that work is merely a platform for evangelism. Evangelistic breakfasts, luncheons and dinners are favored methods of sending missionaries across the canyon, usually with a moving personal conversion story.

The "immigrant" approach: Immigrants move across the canyon and work hard to blend in with fellow workers. However, immigrants often lose their distinct flavor. Their basic belief is that they are powerless to make a difference, must cope with foul language or workplace injustice to survive, and should lay low. While they might take pride in doing a good job, work is something they do mainly for the money. In contrast to the dare devil, who crash-lands at work, the immigrant drops in at church once in a while to try and stay connected.

The "conqueror" approach: Conquerors believe the other side of the canyon is theirs to take back for the Kingdom of God. They want to "get back to the foundation this country was built on." They believe they can expect prosperity if they do things God's way. In other words, biblical values become an instrument for success. Each of these approaches might have some value but we will consider one more.

The "co-worker" approach: Co-workers understand themselves to be co-laborers with God. They know they are created in his image and redeemed through Jesus Christ's atoning death on the cross. They identify with the privilege of working toward the completion of God's plan to bring everything on earth under Christ's control (Ephesians 1:15-23). For example, when a crane operator sets up steel for a new building, he may look at his work with satisfaction, knowing he has worshipped God by bringing order out of chaos.

Moreover, Christian workers are not only God's co-workers, but also co-imagers of God with other workers. Instead of trying to blend in as immigrants, co-workers treat fellow workers, supervisors, and employees with dignity and respect. As redeemed workers, they model something else: the awareness that in all their work, they bring everything under Christ's lordship. As they worship God through work, they influence others for Christ. In this context, they are prepared to give an answer for why they believe. Co-workers believe work is worship, an act of co-laboring with God, and they want fellow-workers to join in worship. The cross is the co-worker's bridge across the canyon. Co-workers feel the strain of living in two worlds at once, yet they dedicate their work to God, believing it is Christ's sanctuary.

Due to a poor theology of work, many workers believe work is merely a platform for verbal witness. Various caricatures of witnessing fail to engage others in authentic conversation about faith in Christ. But the worker who integrates faith through all his work is prepared to explain his faith.

Difficulties with verbal witness

Verbal witness for Christ is difficult in the workplace even for the respected believer. Workers ask questions such as, "How can I witness at work in a way that isn't preachy? Should I share my faith with my boss or with people I supervise?" One worker pointed out that it is difficult to share with people he reports to, because he never knows when he might be discriminated against as a result. Another worker commented that Christians are often perceived as hypocrites, though sometimes he has an opportunity to talk about why he is different.

Finding common ground on which to build relationships with co-workers is another challenge. Some fellow workers are eager to avoid the subject of God. Others are self-conscious and defensive around Christians. For all these reasons and more, being an effective verbal witness at work is very difficult for blue-collar Christians. How then can they overcome barriers and find opportunities to share their faith?

Methods of verbal witness

All that one says gives verbal testimony to his character and beliefs. Redeemed workers express Christ's authority through their words in the workplace. While they are to be prepared to share reasons they believe (1 Peter 3:15), their daily speech also integrates faith at work in three key ways. Words in the workplace reveal credible faith when they have the following characteristics.

First, speech has biblical integrity when it is true (Ephesians 4:25). Blatant lying and subtle deception confront believers in business. White-collar crime depends on deception of both the public and regulators. More subtle forms of lying, such as passing off falsehood as truth, tempt Christians to play along. This presents workers with the following dilemma. When should a Christian blow the whistle on an employer or co-worker if innocent workers could lose their source of income as a result? This is a difficult question, but believers, who are active in the marketplace, must give an honest answer regarding their own performance. Moreover, if asked to lie for the company, workers who do so hurt their own consciences and further weaken the company's moral fabric.

Second, speech has biblical integrity when it is pure (Ephesians 4:29). Unwholesome speech tears others down. The Greek word "sapros" ("unwholesome" in Ephesians 4:29) was applied literally, among other things, to spoiled fish, decayed trees, rotten fruit and worn out shoes.[239] Reineker defines it as "rank, foul, putrid, rotten, worthless, disgusting."[240] An integrated faith, on the other hand, results in speech that builds up listeners. This is the watershed for words: do they contribute to the spiritual and psychological growth of the listener? Conversations need not all be positive. Biblical truth warns against sin's consequences and reveals unpopular facts, but beneficial words have the goal of building people's confidence. Though these verses in Ephesians 4 are directed at speech in the church, integrity in our speech must advance to the marketplace. While in college, I worked salvaging parts for an auto wrecker. My co-workers participated routinely in degrading language and entertainment. When several of us rode to a diner for lunch, the driver played what he called an "inspirational tape," which was a recording of group sex. And in the shop, when a bolt would not loosen or something else went wrong, outburst of creatively linked four-letter words were the norm. Even though I had serious conversations about God with some of my co-workers, I found it difficult not to copy their language when

239 Walter Bauer, *A Greek English Lexicon of the New Testament and Other Early Christian Literature*, 2nd ed., edited by F.W. Gingrich and Frederick Danker (Chicago: University of Chicago Press, 1979), 742.

240 Fritz Rienecker, *A Linguistic Key to the Greek New Testament*, trans. Cleon L. Rogers, Jr. (Grand Rapids: Zondervan, 1982), 534.

a series of things went wrong in my work bay. I needed to persistently anchor my identity and my work in the presence of the Holy Spirit, and even then I found it difficult to keep my speech pure.

Third, speech has biblical integrity when it is kind and not malicious (Ephesians 4:31). The workplace can be a scene of gossip and slander. Talking behind the boss's back, running down another employee, or bad mouthing the staff issues from living out of wounds rather than the healing grace of the Father.

While believing blue-collar workers should prepare to share the truth about Christ, they need the power of the Holy Spirit to help them speak in a way that honors him in daily work. All their speech is a verbal witness, whether they are speaking about Christ or not. Words that have integrity are true, pure and kind.

Finding opportunities for verbal witness

Good effort combined with tolerance for others eventually opens doors for witness. Christian workers are responsible primarily to produce good work and, therefore, no amount of spiritual talk on the job is an excuse for shoddy workmanship.[241] First Corinthians 13 defines how authentic followers of Christ are to live their lives before one another and the world. Faith, hope, and especially love are the signs of success the believer brings to the world.[242] Combining love with good deeds is critical for blue-collar workers who seek opportunities to share their faith. This combination is essential because blue-collar attitudes about belief may be very strong and visceral.

Sample illustrates this, referring to a co-worker who asked him one day as they were laying a pipeline whether Sample believed in the virgin birth or not. He replied, "Well, Snooks, first you've got to compare those passages in the New Testament with those in the Old; then, you've got to look at the cultural context and what it meant to be a divine-human . . ." Snooks interrupted saying, "Wahharr," his favorite expression, "college boy, I didn't ask you what you thought; I asked you what you believed!"[243]

---

241 Henry, *Aspects of Christian Social Ethics*, 70.

242 Smith-Moran, *Soul at Work*, 70.

243 Sample, *Blue-Collar Ministry*, 107.

Christians also cultivate opportunities to share their faith at work when they exhibit hope. For example, in Jesus' parable of the wise and foolish virgins, the wise women knew there would be a delay in the coming of the bridegroom, therefore, they prepared by having enough lamp oil on hand. They had hope and so prepared, but they were not anticipating an imminent evacuation. When we have hope, we are prepared to wait for Christ's return and committed to doing our work well. "Living with hope we know that God will bring the whole human story to a worthwhile end, and even our work in this passing world can last."[244] Anticipating Christ's return propels workers to offer words of hope in conjunction with quality work. The Apostle Paul wrote, "Therefore, my dear brothers, stand firm. Let nothing move you. Always give yourselves fully to the work of the Lord, because you know that your labor in the Lord is not in vain." (1 Cor. 15:58) That work includes verbal witness, but "also includes making widgets, tables, meals and deals."[245]

One other factor in developing opportunities for verbal witness is worth noting here: workers desiring effective witnessing opportunities ought to wait patiently for those opportunities.

> Sometimes the routine of the assembly line permits more occasional conversation with one's fellow worker than does creative work. And the believer, always ready with a reason for his hope, will not be without something to say. The repetition of assembly line operation often gives opportunity for the Christian's friendly interest in the neighbor and for spiritual conversation.[246]

Paul Stevens admits he thought he would have almost daily opportunities to verbally witness for Christ once he moved from pastoral ministry to carpentry. "But," he writes, "it was six weeks on a particular construction job when the dry-wall taper turned to me and asked, 'Paul, what happens when we die?'"[247]

---

244 Stevens, *Doing God's Business*, 213.

245 Ibid., 213

246 Henry, *Aspects of Christian Social Ethics*, 61.

247 Stevens, *Doing God's Business*, 55,56.

Christ's servants need to be patient if they want authentic opportunities to share their faith. Good effort and tolerance with co-workers who hold different views will invite questions about one's beliefs. Workers whose attitudes depict hope are more likely to find occasions to talk about significant spiritual truth with those who learn to trust and respect them.

Jesus Christ mandated that his followers be witnesses for him. Doing so requires workers to be credible co-workers who are prepared to give reasons for their faith. But witness is difficult, even for the prepared. Since speech is the organ of verbal witness, all speech should be considered witness, even words that say nothing explicit about Christ. Furthermore, workers cultivate opportunities to witness through love and good deeds, tolerance, hope and patience.

CHAPTER 15

Women and Blue-collar Work

Women have an increased presence in the blue-collar workforce. Since blue-collar work is dominated by male workers, it can be a difficult environment for women to adapt to.

Women's presence and roles in the workforce have been changing profoundly for several decades. In 1969, the typical American couple worked 5,420 hours a year. The wife worked 2,465 hours per year in the home while her husband worked about 2,955 hours at his job. By 1989, similar couples worked 6,488 hours. The wife worked 1,272 hours at home plus 2,007 in the marketplace, while her husband worked 3,209. In other words, they added the equivalent of one half-time worker. As a result, leisure diminished.[248]

The pressure of balancing hours spent in the work force with household needs continues to challenge working women. In Canada, between 1976 and 2008, the number of weekly work hours declined for men and increased slightly for women. On average, in 2008, men spent 78 minutes less at work, while women spent 30 minutes more at work than they did in 1976.[249] A 2004 report stated that American men worked about an hour more than employed women.[250]

A British survey of 2,000 women who work outside the home found that they spend three hours and fifteen minutes per day preparing for work, three times as long as men, who spend an average of 57

---

248 Shriver, "Hard Work," 540.

249 Statistics Canada. Labour Force Historical Review 2008 (/Table Cd1 Ti0an). Ottawa. Statistics Canada, 2009 (Cat. No. 71F0004XCB).

250 American Time Use Survey—2004. News Release USDL 05-1766.

minutes. Women carry the bulk of the household chores, grocery shopping, getting the children ready for school and seeing that they get there.[251]

One factor benefitting blue-collar women is government intervention that opens jobs for women, who are willing to risk entering the workplace in roles traditionally held by men. These women benefit from good pay and environments where they can learn on the job.[252] This trend continues. One of my sons worked as a laborer in a welding shop where four young women were trained welders. One of the female welders was the lead hand who directed the work of both men and women.

However, blue-collar fields are seldom, if ever, easy for women to adapt to. Trade jobs are mostly an all-male environment.[253] These jobs tend to affirm manhood by offering responsibility for tools, opportunity to use skills, and wages high enough to support the family. In this male dominated context, women who become crusaders for women's rights incite negative treatment. On the other hand, women should be encouraged to speak up when jokes in their workplaces are filled with innuendo or disrespect. When treatment is rude, it is appropriate to report it to management. Furthermore, some injustice against female workers is such that it should be tried in court.[254]

Women in blue-collar jobs also face the question of how to retain femininity in a traditionally male workplace. But femininity is subjective and culturally defined; therefore, it is better to work on principles rather than cultural preferences.

Conversely, some women are staying home from paid employment in order to focus attention on their families and homes. One woman who understood the sacred aspect of her work at home placed this sign over the kitchen sink: "Divine service held here three times daily."[255] Women who see their homes as their work deserve honor as much as those who choose to work away from their homes. Pope John Paul II wrote,

---

251 "Women Spend Twice as Much Time as Men on Chores," *The Daily Telegraph Online*, October 6, 2009.

252 Sample, *Blue-Collar Ministry*, 68,69.

253 Shostak, *Blue-collar Life*, 57.

254 Sherman, *Keeping Your Head Up*, 197.

255 Henry, *Aspects of Christian Social Ethics*, 71.

> It will redound to the credit of society to make it possible for a mother—without inhibiting her freedom, without psychological or practical discrimination, and without penalizing her as compared with other women—to devote herself to taking care of her children and educating them in accordance with their needs, which vary with age. Having to abandon these tasks in order to take up paid work outside the home is wrong from the point of view of the good of society and of the family when it contradicts or hinders these primary goals of the mission of a mother.[256]

One way governments could respond to women who prefer to stay home with their children is to give significant tax advantages to businesses that pay employees well enough that their spouses can choose to stay home. Increasing economic pressure drives many young parents to work, even though the financial benefits are doubtful. In these circumstances, paying for child care reduces the net gain significantly for working mothers. Moreover, the emotional cost to family life is sometimes high.

Women will likely continue to increase in numbers in jobs that were traditionally considered male domains. As they break into new work territory, female blue-collar workers encounter resistance. Where this resistance includes injustice, female workers should be encouraged to fight back through legitimate channels. Other women prefer to stay home with their children. Society should honor this choice as much as the choice to enter the paid workforce.

---

256 Pope Jean Paul II, *Laborem Exercens*, 44.

CHAPTER 16

Authority at Work

Authority. Just saying the word awakens resentment in some people. This is particularly true for blue-collar workers who serve mean-spirited managers. However, workers who have reasonable authority over their own work usually produce better results and enjoy their work.[257]

A Christian view of authority at work

Scripture confirms the authority of human institutions (1 Peter 2:13,14,17). At the same time, Scripture offers a precedent for fair treatment in the workplace. In the Old Testament, slavery was regulated—a major departure from the practice of surrounding cultures (Exodus 12:44; 20:10,21,26f; Deuteronomy 23:16f). God punished masters for oppression of their workers (Jeremiah 22:13f). Therefore, Christian workers are responsible to resist injustice.

> It is certainly not enough to say, as some Christians are fond of saying, that "changed hearts will change society." Racial prejudice may well have begun in individual human hearts, but it has now become institutionalized, codified. It is not enough for individual white people to say, "Now I will begin to treat them differently." Constitutions have

[257] Bakke, *Joy at Work*, 58,59.

> to be rewritten; labor codes have to be changed; jokes and stories must be debunked; self-images need to be repaired; communities have to be rebuilt.[258]

Though Christian workers have a biblical mandate to be subject to those in authority (1 Peter 2:14; Romans 13), they are under greater scriptural authority to honor the Lord. The early Christians often suffered because they did not comply with cultural expectations. They would not worship Caesar but confessed "Jesus is Lord." Submission to authority, as depicted in Romans 13, is balanced by Revelation 13, where the Lord warns the church against obeying governing authorities who blaspheme God.[259] Mouw writes of 1 Peter 2,

> When the Apostle tells us, then, that we are to be subject to government "for the Lord's sake," he is pointing to the element of freedom we have in submitting to institutional authority. Christian subjection is not something a government can assume will be automatically offered. It is something the Christian community offers voluntarily, in full consciousness that it is a choice we make before our Lord.[260]

In the workplace, the Christian worker has freedom before the Lord to do good work for the glory of God. Therefore, when the employer or the union demands the worker act outside of her Christian conviction, she is not subject to their expectations, provided she disagrees or even disobeys with a respectful attitude.

But disobeying authority is an extreme measure that is seldom necessary. Furthermore, griping and complaining against leaders in the workplace antagonizes workers against leaders. Complaining at work, although not a new phenomenon, appears to be on the rise. Reasons for this trend include lack of job security due to global competition, flattened hierarchies, and younger workers who are less

---

258 Mouw, *Called to Holy Worldliness*, 35.

259 Ibid., 61.

260 Ibid., 63.

fearful of managers.[261] "Gallup, a leading U.S. Pollster, reported in August 2007 that 43% of those surveyed were 'completely satisfied' with their jobs. Slightly more than a third said the same about their chances for promotion. Thirty-one per cent said they made enough money. That leaves plenty of margin for let-loose, no-hold-barred belly-aching."[262]

Complaining also results from an "us-them" attitude at work. Dennis Bakke relates how his company took over a 50 year old electrical plant. Management decided to pay year-end bonuses based partially on plant performance. A thirty-year employee named Francis was skeptical about management's motive. Bakke talked to Francis one night as he worked in the control room and said a bonus was likely for everyone in the plant because boiler problems had diminished. Francis merely grunted his conviction that the company would shut the plant down rather than pay bonuses. Nevertheless, just over a month later, the plant manager handed out bonus checks and reminded Francis of his earlier conversation with Bakke. "The boilers didn't get shut down, and you got your bonus," he said cheerily. "Yeah," Francis answered, "but *they* took out taxes."[263] Some workers complain because they are convinced managers are out to get them.

Since Christian workers are subject to the Lord Jesus, they give him the highest level of authority over their lives. At the same time, they are subject to management's authority and must submit to it as long as it does not demand disobedience to God. A key evidence of godly submission is an absence of chronic complaining on the job.

What workers want from managers

Managers impact workers' joy. Unfortunately, in many cases, management is not concerned about workers' sense of well-being. In fact, managers might not willingly trust blue-collar employees with the power to make decisions. However, a work force is motivated when freed to use its abilities and strengths.

God calls managers to serve. But they may be concerned more with convenience than with "sharing the overflowing surplus of divine

261 "We're Just a Bunch of Whiners," *National Post*, 27 June, 2007, WK4.

262 Ibid.

263 Dennis Bakke, *Joy at Work*, (Toronto: Penguin Group, 2005), 171,172.

relationship."[264] "Charged to do 'more with less,' managers have for a variety of reasons become experts at the 'with less' part: less workers, less wages, less benefits, less regulation, less ethics, less security, less time off, less risky creativity, less service, less civility . . ."[265] Furthermore, blue-collar workers may give their best at work but the boss or the workplace culture does not appreciate their contribution. Worse, some bosses give staff a poor performance rating no matter how hard they work.[266] Some blue-collar workers rightly feel they are working for a descendent of Ebenezer Scrooge as depicted in Dickens' *A Christmas Carol.*

> The door of Scrooge's counting-house was open that he might keep his eye upon his clerk who, in a dismal little cell beyond, a sort of tank, was copying letters. Scrooge had a very small fire, but the clerk's fire was so very much smaller that it looked like one coal. But he couldn't replenish it, for Scrooge kept the coal-box in his own room; and so surely as the clerk came in with the shovel, the master predicted that it would be necessary for them to part. Wherefore the clerk put on his white comforter, and tried to warm himself at the candle; in which effort, not being a man of strong imagination, he failed.[267]

Somewhat like Scrooge, some employers fear that trusting employees with opportunities to use their creative abilities, engaging their whole beings at work, will result in lost productivity. However, Hardy cites a study by the U.S. Department of Health, Education, and Wellness which says, "The evidence suggests that meeting the higher needs of workers can, perhaps, increase productivity from 5% to 40%."[268] Similarly, a study by Patrick McVeigh compared the seventy publicly owned companies in the book *The 100 Best*

---

[264] John Dalla Costa, *Magnificence at Work,* (Montreal: Novalis Publishing, 2005), 38.

[265] Ibid.

[266] Sherman, *Keeping Your Head Up,* 193,194.

[267] Charles Dickens, *A Christmas Carol,* quoted in Jane Kise and David Stark, *Working with Purpose,* (Minneapolis: Augsburg, 2004), 150,151.

[268] Hardy, *The Fabric of This World,* 176.

Companies to Work For with the financial performance of Standard and Poor's 500. He found that "the best companies to work for were more than twice as profitable as Standard & Poor's 500; between the years 1975 and 1984, the stock price . . . appreciated at nearly three times the rate of the 500."[269] The importance of serving employees is illustrated by the experience of a large job search company where national marketing consultants spent up to eighty percent of their time traveling; they were away from home most nights. The company suffered poor productivity; employees suffered divorces; job turnover was high. When the company reduced travel time to a forty percent maximum, turnover virtually stopped, and productivity rose to an all-time high.[270]

Workers like a measure of control at their work. For example, Dennis Bakke once asked for a progress report from workers building a porch on his home. Their response was revealing: "Depends on how much time the boss spends here. We get the job done faster when he is away. No one waits around for him to tell us what's next." Bakke concludes, "People become passive under the control of bosses. Ordinary workers need independence and a feeling of control if they are going to take on responsibility, show initiative, and be willing to risk failure."[271] Similarly, Sample quotes Kohn and Schooler.

> Occupational self-direction has the most potent and most widespread effects of all the occupational conditions we have examined. In terms of psychological effects, the central fact of occupational life today . . . is the opportunity to use initiative, thought, and independent judgment in one's work—to direct one's own occupational activities.[272]

Although this is true, many blue-collar jobs permit little creative thought. In some cases, creativity would spell disaster. For example, there is only one way to fit a two hundred pound, twenty foot length of pipe into the collar of another pipe. One veteran worker yelled to his young, college-educated co-worker, "Hey, college boy, this ain't like

---

269 Ibid.

270 Ibid., 177.

271 Bakke, *Joy at Work*, 58,59.

272 Sample, *Blue-Collar Ministry*, 90.

it is in school. You can't do it any way you want to. And yore opinion don't mean a damned thing. There's a right way, and all the other ways are wrong. If you don't do it right, you can't do it."[273]

Still, where feasible, workers want freedom to use their strengths—to be persons! A laborer whose welding shop experience was demeaning and depersonalizing moved on to another job when the welding shop closed down. At the new job, adults were treated like adults; they were free to decide when to take coffee breaks; some voluntarily stayed late in order to complete the work of the day.[274] The link between personal respect and productivity was obvious.

Unfortunately, this atmosphere is not the norm, as Nash observes. "From a self-interest business viewpoint, however, a manager's psychological orientation is stunted at the start. Other people's needs and interests are perceived only in terms of their capacity to enhance or inhibit one's own interests."[275]

Managers are not the enemy, but they are often motivated by enormous pressure to make their departments succeed. Conjointly, they do not find it easy to trust workers to make decisions or take initiative. Yet to encourage good morale and productivity, managers must learn to allow workers the freedom, whenever possible, to make decisions and use their best strengths.

Are labor unions the solution to authority issues?

Are unions past their usefulness? If so, why do workers join them? When they function well, they promote just practices in the workplace. Unfortunately, this is not always the case. Where have they gone wrong and how might they be of use in the future?

Workers still join unions, but today only 12% of the labor force in the U.S. is unionized.[276] Fear of exploitation by management is a major reason why workers join unions. However, according to a senior human resources leader in a large Canadian company,

---

273 Ibid., 77.

274 Conversation with a laborer. 2008.

275 Nash, *Good Intentions Aside*, 97.

276 "Economist Expects Core Inflation to Lift," *National Post*, 31 July, 2008, FP4.

> Management tends to see unions as living in the past, perpetuating an out-moded adversarial relationship with management. Union leadership is weak and focuses on protecting the mediocre 20 percent of members. But if there were no unions, would management exploit their workers? Probably.[277]

Unions ought to promote justice at work. Christians formed the first unions in order to fight exploitation, particularly in the mills and mines of Britain, but as secular values gained power, the adversarial approach became their default position.[278] "Nevertheless," writes Sutherland, "we believe that there is a Christian way of doing labor relations. First, what ought our objective to be as a Christian union—'more and ever more' or something better? . . . Our goal is to promote just practices in the workplace."[279] In other words, both workers and employers must be flexible and innovative in order to achieve "productivity, fair wages and job stability."[280]

The Bible acknowledges the temptation of those with power to take advantage of those who are vulnerable. As a case in point, de-unionization in the U.S. widened the pay gap between executives and workers by a jaw-dropping margin. "Between 1980 and 1992, for instance, average executive pay rose by 511 percent, compared to 63 percent for workers' wages. Inflation during that period was 70 percent."[281] Scripture warns those in authority against misusing their power (Leviticus 25:43, 53; Colossians 4:1).

Where, in the midst of this disparity, have unions gone wrong? They have neglected vital aspects that are important to workers, aspects such as input into company decision-making.[282]

---

277 John Sutherland, "Who Needs Unions? We do!" in *The Marketplace*, September/October, 1995, 20.

278 John Sutherland, "A Union Run by Christians," in *The Marketplace*, July/August, 2000, 11.

279 Ibid.

280 Ibid.

281 Ibid.

282 Grootenboer, *About Work and Unions*, 11.

> Many unions have adapted very well to being only skillful adversaries of management. It is too bad that at the same time they have deprived themselves and their members of an effective and meaningful role in the operation of the enterprise. One of the consequences is that both labor and management focus all their attention on the dollar value of work.[283]

The roots of unions' failures to engender meaningful change in the workplace have to do with their Marxist philosophy—their entrenched view that life is a class struggle between "haves" and "have-nots".[284]

Perhaps the chief contribution the Christian faith can make to the workplace environment is to painstakingly build community. Christian workers can learn to lead cooperative efforts between managers and co-workers. Matsushita Electric Company of Japan illustrates integration of spirituality and work.

> The company's founder] adopted a code of seven spiritual values as the basis for operating his company. This type of corporate philosophy can only be effective in the context of a cooperative community. We are learning from the Japanese that many of the values they have applied so successfully are similar to the values and principles in our Western religious tradition but which we have mistakenly kept separate from our work environment, with a consequent dehumanizing of work and the stifling of our human potential.[285]

In order to be relevant in a changing workplace, unions must see and address not only workers' wages but also their need for participation in the planning process.

Union leaders and managers also ought to look beyond entrenched stereotypes and political positions to find mutual ground, and that ground should be the all-round well-being of the workers.

---

283 Grootenboer, *About Work and Unions*, 10.

284 Ibid., 6.

285 Tucker, *Us and Them*, 70.

Scripture teaches blue-collar workers to be subject to legitimate authority at work. This subjection is voluntary, out of reverence for Christ, who is Lord of the workplace. As responsible adults, workers want input into the procedures that affect their own lives at work. Generally, unions have failed to address this issue; however, they may yet choose to become more effective if they see beyond the issues of political power and money.

CHAPTER 17

Rest

Plutarch said, "Rest is the sweet sauce of the soul." Yet, why would Christian blue-collar workers rest, and is there a biblical foundation for doing so?

A personal account of rest

I remember when, as a child of 9 or 10, I did my homework on a Sunday afternoon. The farmhouse was quiet that day. My dad sat in the corner chair resting from hard, physical work. In hindsight, I realize he was resting from the stress of a farm economy that paid less as costs climbed. When my mother returned home from visiting someone and asked what we had been up to, Dad said he was not sure he wanted to say what I had been doing. He was not scolding me, but I knew he felt uncomfortable because, as a family, we were not observing the Sabbath as his early training insisted we should. As he saw it, school work tarnished the holy day that was set apart from all kinds of work. However, today most Christians do not give working, shopping or sporting on Sunday a second thought. For most people, the pendulum has swung far from strict rules to an easy-going disregard for religious observation of a day of rest.

Rest in the Old Testament

God rested from his work of creation, and he declared the seventh day a holy day. Genesis 2:1-3 says, "So the creation of the heavens and the earth and everything in them was completed. On the seventh day, having finished his task, God rested from all his work. And God blessed the seventh day and declared it holy, because it was the day when he rested from his work of creation." (Genesis 2:1-3, NLT) God blessed the day after he completed creation, giving Sabbath as a gift. The Hebrew word "bless" means to endue with power for success, prosperity and longevity among other things.[286]

God also instituted Sabbath as an opportunity to remember his gift of redemption (Deuteronomy 5:12-15; cf. Exodus 20:8-11). Furthermore, Exodus 31:17 says the Sabbath is a permanent sign of God's covenant with Israel because God rested on the seventh day and was refreshed. "The language is purposely strong so that man may learn the necessity of regarding the Sabbath as a day on which he himself is to rest from his daily labors."[287]

The Old Testament reveals an additional reason for Sabbath. Israel was to give servants a day to rest so that they did not work every day. Israel's attitude toward slaves was tempered by the fact that they could remember the hardship of slavery in Egypt (Deuteronomy 5:14).[288]

Rest in the New Testament

Jesus changed the direction of history by securing, through his blood, a new covenant with God (1 Corinthians 11:25). Hebrews chapters three and four illustrate this change and show God's plan to give his people a kind of rest not realized by Israel, which had failed to enter God's rest because of its unbelief (Hebrews 4:3,4). By contrast, Christian workers look forward to a place of rest promised through Christ. As a result, they obey the word of God (Hebrews 4:10-13), and they rely on Christ as their Great High Priest, who understands human weakness and who will give grace to overcome temptation (Hebrews 4:11-16).

Rest gives workers time to withdraw from work so they can acknowledge God as Creator and Ruler of the universe. Rest also acknowledges that all time belongs to God. Sabbath-rest is to time as tithing is to finance—it acknowledges that the whole belongs to God.

---

[286] John N. Oswalt, "beraka," in *Theological Wordbook of the Old Testament,* 1:132.

[287] E. J. Young and F. F. Bruce, "Sabbath," in *New Bible Dictionary,* ed. J. D. Douglas, (Leicester: Inter-Varsity, 1962), 1042.

[288] Ibid.

One day set aside specifically to worship helps workers remember that every work day is sacred. So we see that God's rest refers to confidence that he is Lord and Savior in all of life and that those who trust him will some day be with him in glorious perfection.

What Old Testament Sabbath regulations could not do, Christ has done by introducing workers to God and giving them certainty of rest when this life's work is complete. Therefore, Christian workers can approach work with an attitude that acknowledges Christ as their ultimate hope. This, in itself, can be a source of peace in a turbulent workplace. " . . . God's people of the new covenant are exhorted to claim now the ancient promise of God's rest, available to them in Jesus Christ, and to lay hold of it in hope, by faith in Christ our Lord."[289]

Jesus contradicted the religious teachers' abuses of Sabbath law. Although Jesus kept the Sabbath according to Old Testament regulations, he identified *himself* as Lord of the Sabbath (Mark 2:28). He disregarded the oral tradition that burdened people with details. But he did not attack the institution of the Sabbath as such. Rather, he opposed the Pharisees who nullified the word of God with their extra teaching.[290] So, Jesus redeemed Sabbath as a gift for people rather than enforcing Sabbath as a burden.

Furthermore, Jesus modeled rest. In Mark 6:30-32 Jesus invited his disciples to "come with me by yourselves to a quiet place and get some rest." Moreover, Jesus emphasized the importance of rest and reflection when he affirmed Mary's decision to sit at his feet rather than busy herself with meal preparation (Luke 10:38-42).

Rest and the teaching of the church

While Jesus redeemed rest for his people, the church has often emphasized aspects of Old Testament Sabbath. The early church began to meet on Sunday, the first day of the week instead of Saturday, the Jewish Sabbath. Although the New Testament does not reveal why the church met on Sunday, several reasons have been suggested: They did not regard Saturday as a day they had to observe as Sabbath; Christ rose from the dead on Sunday; New Testament

---

289 R. Hensel, C. Brown, "Rest," in *Dictionary of New Testament Theology*, Vol. 3. 257.

290 Young and Bruce, "Sabbath," 1043.

writers consistently referred to Sunday as the day Christ rose again and appeared to his disciples; God sent the Holy Spirit on Pentecost, a Sunday; Christians may have anticipated that Christ's return would take place on a Sunday; The church may have wanted to distinguish itself from Judaism.[291]

However, churches have often chosen one of three approaches to Sabbath rest. Some believe the church was wrong to replace Saturday with Sunday as a day of worship and rest. These churches, notably Seventh-day Adventists, preserve Saturday as the Sabbath day. Others transfer many of the strict Sabbath rules to Sunday. Theologians of the fourth and fifth centuries identified the so-called "Christian Sabbath" with the Jewish Sabbath.[292] Many Christians adopt a third view, which sees Sabbath rest as an attitude of worship with less emphasis on the particular day.

Implications of rest for blue-collar workers

Although Jesus functioned in the context of Old Testament Sabbath, he did not command his followers to observe Sabbath in the order of the Old Testament. On the contrary, the Jewish authorities despised him for his apparent disregard for their extra-Sabbath regulations. Furthermore, Paul exhorts Christians to resist the condemnation of those who would judge them with regard to Sabbath observance: "Therefore do not let anyone judge you by what you eat or drink, or with regard to a religious festival, a New Moon celebration or a Sabbath day. These are a shadow of the things that were to come; the reality, however, is found in Christ." (Colossians 2:16,17) While the worker is not constricted by Old Testament law, what aspects of rest, other than the opportunity for a day off, should the church promote to workers?

First, since workers are created in the image of God, who rested from his work, they may justifiably take time to rest and reflect on his goodness, exhibited in creation. If God as a worker influences one's view of the value of work, then God's rest invites those made in his image to rest.

---

291 D.K. Lowery, "Lord's Day," in *Evangelical Dictionary of Theology*, ed. Walter A. Elwell. (Grand Rapids: Baker, 1984), 649.

292 F. R. Harm, "Sabbatarianism," in *Evangelical Dictionary of Theology*, 963.

Second, Christian workers approach daily responsibilities with the awareness that every day is holy. This principle emerges from our previous reference to Hebrews three and four. While workers anticipate rest from labor at the end of their work on earth, they may translate that confidence into the tasks at hand, knowing that Christ has already promised rest. This promise does not *prescribe* a day of rest, but it does instill an attitude of confidence because Christian workers anticipate perfect rest.

Third, rest from work interrupts the cycle of working in order to acquire things. "Like God's rest, leisure frees us from the need for productivity, and allows us instead to enjoy what has already been made. It has within it the quality of 'letting go' of the utilitarian urges that occupy us in the world of getting and spending."[293] Through rest, workers celebrate what they have accomplished and enjoy the things they've gained instead of continually yearning for more.

Fourth, rest recognizes human dignity.[294] Allowing time to rest dignifies the worker as more than a tool or instrument through which to accomplish work.

Finally, Scripture refers to several related values of rest and reflection: beauty for the sake of beauty is a wonderful thing (Psalm 19:1f); God's holiness is beautiful to reflect on (Psalm 29:2); God's sanctuary is beautiful (Psalm 96:6); the beautiful flowers are considered as an example of rest and faith (Matthew 6:25-34).[295] Rest aids contemplation.

Blue-collar workers have sound reasons to respect the importance of rest. Workers benefit from taking a regular day off from work. Doing so not only restores them physically, but also spiritually.

---

293 Ryken, *Work and Leisure in Christian Perspective*, 183.

294 Kaiser, *Theology of Work*, 50.

295 Kaiser, *Theology of Work*, 184.

CHAPTER 18

Job Selection and Gifts

Workers may not be interested in discovering or developing their gifts because they are too busy surviving their jobs. Moreover, supervisors usually care about getting work done more than fulfilling a worker's sense of accomplishment. Nevertheless, Christ's followers bring glory to God when they nurture the colorful variety of their gifts.

Although gifts alone do not indicate which job is most appropriate for a worker, gifts are still relevant considerations for job selection. Whenever possible, workers should try to find work that harnesses their gifts. If they have the ability to do a repetitive task but little else, they should continue to do so. But if they have creative gifts that equip them to do something else, they should seek to find that other work.[296] What's more, work that matches a believer's gifts maximizes achievement and potential witness for Christ.[297]

Furthermore, Christians should not become pastors if their gifts and abilities make a greater difference in the marketplace than through serving on a church staff. Neither should pastors press everyone to become an ordained minister. For instance, a laborer who understands the workings of an oil rig contributes to God's kingdom by using his strengths in his workplace. Urging him to become a pastor may well lead to embarrassment and pain for him and for the church of Jesus Christ.[298] Baxter complained that well-meaning parents have directed

296 Henry, *Aspects of Christian Social Ethics*, 61.

297 Ryken, *Work and Leisure in Christian Perspective*, 173.

298 Henry, *Aspects of Christian Social Ethics*, 69.

their children toward career ministry even when they were not fit for the role.[299]

So, a person who is mentally or physically unable to take on a particular role needs to know himself in order to choose work that will benefit not only the public good but also his own health. This is so, not only of the role of a pastor but of any "great work" or "holy office" to borrow Baxter's terms. Job seekers must be honest about the gifts, skills, and limitations that God has given them.

Being aware of one's gifts is useful to the job search, yet gifts may not ultimately be the determining factor in job selection. Some mistakenly assume that identifying their spiritual gifts is synonymous with entering career ministry. This is not the case. Most gifts can be used in the context of the marketplace.

---

299 Richard Baxter, "Directions About Our Labour and Callings," 285.

CHAPTER 19

Meaning and Work

Workers often feel alienated from their work. Is this because some work is truly meaningless? Jesus Christ confronts this common workplace perspective. Moreover, God as Creator calls people of faith to meaningful work that develops character and glorifies God. Yet when should a Christian worker consider changing jobs?

Workers feel alienated from their work

When workers cannot see or experience the results of their work, they often feel alienated from their jobs. Work loses meaning when it is only a source of money to pay for workers' lifestyles. Furthermore, workers who are far removed from the people who use their products have a difficult time seeing their work as ministry. A shoe repairman, because he meets his customers face to face, is more likely to see his work as ministry than the factory worker who stamps steel every day. Each of these people's work eventually impacts others.[300] Yet, when a person spends his work week doing something he cannot see as beneficial to others, he begins to feel cynical about the work.[301]

Those who manufacture things that feed the consumer market often question the meaning of their work. Dorothy Sayers contends that workers should demand work that is both meaningful and useful.[302] Her conviction might be idealistic. Nevertheless, her point

300 Diehl, *The Monday Connection*, 38.

301 Haughey, *Converting Nine to Five*, 17.

302 Sayers, *Creed or Chaos*, 55.

is that workers deserve to do worthwhile things. She writes, "The greatest insult which a commercial age has offered to the worker has been to rob him of all interest in the end-product of the work and to force him to dedicate his life to making badly things which were not worth making."[303]

The sense that others do not appreciate one's work is as discouraging as producing things no one needs. A friend complained that he "bends over backwards" for a customer who then buys from another supplier anyway. As a result, my friend described his work as an emotional roller coaster.[304]

Companies can also leave one feeling that her work is meaningless. Alienated workers feel like instruments owned but not valued. Haughey cites bureaucracy, specialized division of labor, the threat of mergers and acquisitions (and therefore job loss), automation and technology, discrimination and the internationalization of the economy as causes for alienation at work. He writes, "Those afflicted usually turn in on themselves in some way. These inward turns take the form of cynicism or inferiority or despair or hostility or a sense of fatalism."[305]

In contrast, even one expression of support can affirm another person's value at work. For example, after giving an interview, William Diehl affirmed the reporter who interviewed him, thanking her for her ministry. When she asked what he meant, he explained that she would minister to him and her readers if she accurately represented him. A prolonged conversation followed, during which she admitted leaving her church out of disillusionment. Years later, the journalist told Diehl that each time she wrote an article she recalled his encouragement. And, as a result she had reconnected with her church.[306]

Being far removed from the consequences of their work, many people feel their jobs lack meaning. Additionally, when one produces things he does not value, he feels discouraged. Workers commonly feel they are not valued by either customers or companies. This raises the question, "Do all jobs have meaning?"

---

303 Ibid., 56.

304 Conversation with a sales representative, 2007.

305 Haughey, *Converting Nine to Five*, 31.

306 Diehl, *The Monday Connection*, 39 40.

Is some work truly meaningless?

What if the only job a worker can find seems frivolous? Should he take the job or look for something with more obvious impact for the kingdom of God? Some jobs seem to fail as places of worship no matter how hard one works. The sale of furry dice, for example, may seem meaningless.[307] But economics may dictate what work is available. If selling furry dice is the only job one can get to help support the family, she had better take it and do the work for the glory of God. Moreover, the disabled adult who works in the hospital gift shop, selling cards and knickknacks gives her best effort for the glory of God.

On the other hand, if one has the option of doing something more suitable to her gifts, as we have already seen, she should do so. Generally, workers bring meaning to the work they do by doing the work for the glory of God. A man in England who wanted to become a pastor, and so began his seminary training, illustrates this principle. In order to pay his school bills he took a break from studies and took a job in a brewery. Year after year, he put off going back to seminary and continued working in the beer-making business. He loved his co-workers, encouraged them and led many of them to Christ. Finally, after many years of this work, he completed his education. On his ordination Sunday a bus load of co-workers from the brewery arrived at the church. One after another testified how this man, as their godly co-worker, had influenced them to become followers of Jesus. While most Christians probably would not choose to make beer as a way to glorify God, he may lead an individual to bring meaning to unlikely places.

Should workers measure work's meaning by its obvious impact on souls? A volunteer at a church learning center worked only part time serving tables at a restaurant in order to have as much time as possible to work at the learning center. He valued the more obvious ministry at the learning center over the service job of waiting tables. While most people applauded his decision, Dennis Bakke questions his belief that the learning center was more important than serving tables.

---

307 Sherman, *Keeping Your Head Up*, 85.

> With his attitude and philosophy about work, was he really doing justice to his job at the restaurant? Was he treating the role of waiter as one ordained by God? Was he performing his job as God's steward serving the dozens of people who sat in his area of the restaurant each night? Was he cutting corners? Did he have a godly attitude? If he didn't see his work as a sacred responsibility, would he do his best? Would his light shine brightly for God, or would he go through the motions to earn money and save his best efforts for the learning center?[308]

Solomon addressed the apparent meaninglessness of work. But, he also described work as a means of satisfaction and as a gift from God.

> What does a man get for all the toil and anxious striving with which he labors under the sun? All his days his work is pain and grief; even at night his mind does not rest. This too is meaningless. A man can do nothing better than to eat and drink and find satisfaction in his work. This too, I see, is from the hand of God, for without him, who can eat or find enjoyment? (Ecclesiastes 2:22-25)

How can one apply this principle to daily tasks? Personally, I dislike cleaning up the back yard in the spring. The mold left behind after the snow melts makes me sneeze; the garbage blown in from who knows where is annoying; picking up after the family dog was disgusting. Still, while the job is not pleasant, cleaning the yard is an opportunity to worship the Lord with a grateful heart. I am thankful for spring and signs of life after the yard appeared frozen and dead through another long winter. I participate in making this little space more productive; I help create an environment for renewal in the coming months, a place for family barbecues, visits around the fire, enjoying the beauty of flowers and the flavor of chives and fresh tomatoes. Therefore, I give it my best because in some way, my work has an impact on the future.

---

308 Bakke, *Joy at Work*, 253,254.

While some jobs, on the surface, appear frivolous, they might offer the only work available. Workers bring meaning to their jobs even when those jobs are not obvious "ministries." Although workers may legitimately search for work that best uses their gifts, they should not despise work that appears less "spiritual." Instead, Jesus calls workers to see work as a gift of God and a source of satisfaction.

Working with the Creator adds meaning to work

Workers can find meaning in work, whether paid or free, when they serve the Creator. Moreover, they add meaning to their jobs as they give their best effort to make the world a better place. Because they are created in the image of God, he mandates them to bring the earth and everything in it into subjection.[309] Droel and Pierce argue, "The first aim of work is to bring creation toward perfection."[310] They continue, "If one's work is service, then those services must be brought to successful completion: administering therapy, serving a meal, giving a lecture, or finishing the family laundry."[311] Doing work well goes hand in glove with the process of personal growth and development. Sayers adds, "The only Christian work is good work well done. Let the Church see to it that the workers are Christian people and do their work well, as to God: then all the work will be Christian work, whether it is Church-embroidery or sewage farming."[312] John Stott shares a letter he received from a man who found satisfaction in serving the Creator. The man wrote that working to serve himself did not please him. But his letter also said, "I like to think that I am responsible for a part of the greater field pattern whereby all serve human welfare and obey the will of our wonderful Creator."[313]

---

309 Droel and Pierce, *Confident and Competent*, 42.

310 Ibid., 44.

311 Ibid.

312 Sayers, *Creed or Chaos*, 58.

313 John Stott, "Reclaiming the Biblical Doctrine of Work," *Christianity Today*, 4 May, 1979, quoted in Ryken, *Work and Leisure in Christian Perspective*, 171.

Meeting practical needs gives meaning to work

Blue-collar workers serve God by meeting people's practical needs. Pope Jean Paul II noted that work can result in an orderly society; therefore, work impacts the kingdom of God. In other words, by serving others, blue-collar workers serve God when they improve the lives of other people.[314]

However, serving God through work does not ensure one's job will be pleasurable. On the contrary, work can grind the mind, and dull the emotions. When this is the case, at least workers can legitimately value work as a means of earning a living. Hauerwas, as previously noted, wrote,

> While it may be true that any kind of work may have periods of intrinsic pleasure and interest—i.e. bricklaying, running a punch press, writing, painting—nonetheless most work is not intrinsically fulfilling, but a necessity for survival as well as contributing to our interdependence as social beings.[315]

Workers may sometimes consider changing jobs. First, when workers cannot maintain themselves and their dependents, necessity forces them to consider other work. Second, if one may do more public good by serving in a different capacity, that person should move to a different role.[316]

These details about the meaning of work provide a background for the following questions jobseekers might ask themselves:

- What is the mission of this company and how could I help fulfill it?
- Will this mission motivate me to do quality work?

---

314 The Second Vatican Ecumenical Council, Pastoral Constitution on the Church in the Modern World, "Gaudium et Spes," 39:AAs 58, 1966, quoted in Hauerwas, "Work as Co-creation: A Critique of a Remarkably Bad Idea," in *Co-Creation and Capitalism*, eds. Houck and Oliver, 60.

315 Hauerwas, "Work as Co-Creation," in *Co-Creation and Capitalism*, eds. Houck and Oliver, 48.

316 Perkins, "A Treatise on the Vocations," 272.

- Where can my skills add value to this workplace?
- Will I be able to acknowledge this job as a gift from God and be thankful for it?
- Will this job provide an outlet for my gifts and skills?
- What skills, both technical and interpersonal, will I need to develop in order to do this job?
- What sector of society or group of people will I be serving through this job?
- How will my work improve their lives?
- How might this job challenge my faith? Am I ready for this challenge?

In summary, blue-collar workers often feel alienated from their work. When work has little apparent meaning or when the job is unappreciated, workers might feel their jobs are meaningless. But Jesus Christ transforms one's view of work by first transforming the worker. Awareness of one's role as a created, called participant in the Kingdom of God reveals one's work as meaningful. Finally, workers ascribe meaning to work through meeting practical needs and earning a living.

CHAPTER 20

Prayer at Work

Prayer is relevant to the workplace. Workers who embrace Christ as Lord of their entire lives make prayer a central feature of work. In fact, they see work as Christ's sanctuary.

Prayer to the Lord of the workplace

When workers embrace Christ as Lord of the workplace, they incorporate prayer into their job sites. In an age when strategic planning is vital to the survival of business and family finance, prayer is a neglected, yet equally essential facet of business and personal wholeness. The believer who acknowledges God's creative presence at work makes prayer a companion of his gifts and talents.

Incorporating prayer into the workplace is a practical way to address the tension of living as citizens of both heaven and earth. Laborers can make the workplace a place of continual prayer. For example, the tradesman gifted in serving can pray over each piece of plumbing, asking God to bless both the work of his hands and the people who will live in the house he plumbs. Because Christ is Lord of all aspects of Christian life, prayer becomes a companion to one's gifts and responsibilities at work.

Work as Christ's sanctuary for prayer

A Christian worker integrates prayer with his job when he regards his place of work as Christ's sanctuary. But many churches declare an alternative world view when a worship leader, pastor or elder welcomes the people to "The House of the Lord." In other words, church leaders sometimes project the idea that church buildings are more holy than other places. This perception persists despite biblical emphasis that God's *people* are his sanctuary. One could say that God dwells in church buildings, since God is Lord everywhere. But one must acknowledge God's people as the unique dwelling of God (1 Corinthians 3:16; 6:19).

Christians should also acknowledge that God, as Creator and Redeemer of all things, is the rightful owner of every physical structure. Therefore, they can consecrate the ship yard, the rig deck, the kitchen, and the shop floor to him. For example, Christian monks view work as prayer; "To work is to pray," they say. Likewise, workers can seize moments at work and turn them into opportunities for meditation.[317]

Yet, in practice, workers seldom regard their jobs as sanctuaries of prayer. In fact, they may view prayer and the workplace as polar opposites. Teilhard de Chardin comments on the attitude some have toward the spiritual relevance of work.

> I don't think I am exaggerating when I say that nine out of ten practicing Christians feel that man's work is always at the level of a spiritual encumbrance. In spite of the practice of right intentions, and the day offered every morning to God, the general run of the faithful dimly feel that the time spent at the office or the studio, in the fields or in the factory, is time spent away from prayer and adoration.[318]

Christ is Lord of the workplace; it is his sanctuary. Therefore, work is not the opposite of prayer; work and prayer are two hands of the same body. Wingren writes, "God is Creator, and he steadily brings forth new creations giving new forms to the exercise of the vocations of men. Therefore man must always keep the door open for God, as in hesitancy and desperation he seeks guidance from God through prayer . . ."[319] In other words, God's creative power continues to operate in the workplace, and workers acknowledge this through prayer.

---

317 Thomas Moore, *A Life At Work*, (New York: Broadway Books, 2008), 167.
318 Droel and Pierce, *Confident and Competent*, 47.
319 Wingren, *The Christian's Calling*, 184.

The practice of prayer at work

How can workers practice prayer in a workplace that may be volatile, aggressive, and verbally abusive? By growing in Christ-like character. In the following chart, Sherman contrasts the impact of Christ-like character with self-centeredness.

	When comfort and convenience matter most . . .	*When Christ-like character matters most . . .*
You'll pray:	"Lord, make this problem go away."	"Lord, not my will but Yours be done; only help me learn to respond correctly."
You'll think:	Why is God doing this to me? When will it be over? I'm angry at God for allowing this.	I must trust in God's good purpose and plan for me, and learn to depend on Him more.
You'll value:	Being in control of your circumstances; trusting in yourself; achievement, prestige, and peer respect.	Being dependent on God daily; a deep relationship with God that affects all other relationships; the character He is building into you.
You'll experience:	Frustration and anger because your goals are blocked.	A daily walk with Christ that involves Him in the details of your life.
Your character will be:	Superficial, self-centered, bitter, and arrogant.	That of a Christ-like servant who both knows and trusts God in his or her daily experience.[320]

Ralston Young illustrated a prayer-filled life at work. He was a black man known as Red Cap Number 42 at his job as a porter at New York's Grand Central Station. He had been a moody young man after he moved to New York in 1920; he was disillusioned and bored with booze and immorality. Through the influence of an elderly lady, who began taking his niece to Sunday school, Ralston began attending church. There, he " . . . learned about a man who died to take away the sins of the world. He became convinced that any man could become fearless, compassionate, and unconquerable, and could live without grudges or prejudice if he followed the Nazarene."[321] Eventually, Ralston felt there should be a gathering place for believers in the Grand Central neighborhood, and received permission to use an empty coach on Track 13. From that point on, Monday, Wednesday and Friday noon found Ralston welcoming as few as four and as many as twelve executives, clerks, professionals, jobless wanderers, rich and poor to the prayer group. For fifteen minutes, after reciting The Lord's Prayer together, they would

> . . . pray for the peace of the world; the ending of industrial warfare; the settlement of racial and religious strife; and the resolution of their own personality problems. They confided in each other their successes and failures as they sought to pattern their lives after that of the Master. If Ralston brought some troubled traveler along, they talked of his problems, too. Finally, they offered thanks for the help God had given them in the last twenty-four hours. Then they scattered to offices, stores, and sidewalks, feeling strengthened and invigorated.[322]

But Ralston also prayed with travelers individually and encouraged them. While standing beside the wheelchair of a tiny, silver-haired woman, he noticed she was crying. After removing his red cap and closing his eyes, he opened them again and complemented the woman's hat and dress. The old woman smiled as she saw his

---

320 Sherman, *Keeping Your Head Up*, 110,111.

321 Sam Shoemaker et al., *Steps to a New Beginning*, (Nashville: Thomas Nelson, 1993), 37.

322 Sam Shoemaker et al., *Steps to a New Beginning*, 39,40.

empathetic face and asked what made him say that to her. "The good Lord," he replied. Momentarily, she apologized for breaking down as she had but explained that she was in pain all the time. "Can you imagine what that is like?" she asked him.

> "Yes, ma'am. I had to lose an eye—and for years afterward it hurt me like a hot iron."
> "How were you ever able to endure it?"
> "Just praying."
> "Did prayer take your pain away?"
> "No, ma'am. But it brought me the strength to stand the pain."

Ralston never saw the woman again but a year later, hearing a voice page Number 42, he went to the Information Desk and was greeted by the woman's daughter. "Before my mother died," she said, "she asked me to find you and tell you that what you said last summer made all the difference in the world to her."[323]

Prayer at work furthers the creative work of God. Although workers seldom have freedom to pray out loud whenever they want to, they may learn to practice prayer at work. Some jobs, like Ralston Young's, present obvious opportunities for prayer, while only silent prayer is appropriate in other jobs.

In any case, prayer has a place in the blue-collar workplace. Christ-centered thinking is the platform for prayer at work. And for the worker who wants to glorify the Lord at work, prayer may be silent and private or, occasionally, loud and public.

---

323 Ibid., 34-39.

About the Author

Grant McDowell is a past president of the Leduc Regional Chamber of Commerce. He has been a pastor for over thirty years, and tries to integrate faith in daily life wherever he can. His doctoral work at Gordon-Conwell Theological Seminary was in the area of Christianity in the Workplace.

Bibliography

Allen, Ronald B. "asab," In *Theological Wordbook of the Old Testament.* Vol. 2, 687-688. Edited by R. Laird Harris, Gleason L. Archer, Jr., Bruce K. Waltke. Chicago: Moody, 1980.

American Time Use Survey Online—2004. News Release USDL 05-1766.

Antonides, Harry. "From Confrontation to Partnershi" In *Labour of Love,* 105-119. Edited by Josina Van Nuis Zylstra. Toronto: Wedge Publishing, 1980.

Aristotle. Eudemian Ethics, I.IV.2. Quoted in Laura Nash, *Good Intentions Aside,* 24. Boston: Harvard Business School Press, 1993.

Bakke, Dennis. *Joy at Work.* Toronto: Penguin Group, 2005.

Bang, Sunki. "Tensions in Witness." *Vocatio,* July 1998, 17-18. Quoted in Paul Stevens, *Doing God's Business.* Grand Rapids: Eerdmans, 2006.

Banks, Robert. "The Place of Work in the Divine Economy." In *Faith Goes to Work,* 18-29. Edited by Robert Banks. New York: The Alban Institute, 1993.

________., ed. *Faith Goes to Work, Reflections from the Marketplace.* New York: The Alban Institute, 1993.

Barnette, Henlee H. *Christian Calling and Vocation*. Grand Rapids: Baker, 1965.

Bauer, Walter. *A Greek English Lexicon of the New Testament and Other Early Christian Literature*. 2nd ed. Edited by F.W. Gingrich and Frederick Danker. Chicago: University of Chicago Press, 1979.

Baxter, Richard. "Directions About Our Labour and Callings." In *Callings*, 278-285. Edited by William C. Placher. Grand Rapids: Eerdmans, 2005.

Bernbaum, John A. and Steer, Simon M. *Why Work? Careers and Employment in Biblical Perspective*. Grand Rapids: Baker Book House, 1986.

Blanchard, Kenneth H. "Motivational Factors Test For Managers." Quoted in Pine Tree Management Skills Inc., *Management Skills For Front Line Managers*, (seminar taught in Edmonton, Alberta), Module 1.

Burns, Camilla. "The Call of Creation." In *Revisiting the Idea of Vocation*, 24-40. Edited by John C. Haughey, S. J. Washington: Catholic University of America Press, 2004.

Chen, Marvin Yaotsu and Regan, Thomas. *Work in the Changing Canadian Society*. Toronto: Butterworths, 1985.

Colson, Charles and Eckerd, Jack. *Why America Doesn't Work*. Dallas: Word, 1991

Coombs, Marie Theresa. *Called by God*. Collegeville: Liturgical Press, 1992.

Dalla Costa, John. *Magnificence at Work*. Montreal: Novalis Publishing, 2005.

Dennis, Maxine. "Compassion is the Most Vital Tool of my Trade." In Pierce, *Of Human Hands*, 49-51. Edited by Gregory F. Augustine Pierce. Minneapolis: Augsburg, 1991.

Dickens, Charles. *A Christmas Carol.* Quoted in Jane Kise and David Stark, *Working with Purpose*, Minneapolis: Augsburg, 2004.

Diehl, William. *The Monday Connection.* San Francisco: Harper, 1991.

Droel, William L. and Pierce, Gregory F. Augustine. *Confident and Competent.* Notre Dame, IN: Ave Maria Press, 1987.

"Economist Expects Core Inflation to Lift." *National Post*, 31 July, 2008, FP4.

"Elizabeth May's Bizarre Speech." *National Post Online*, 1 May, 2007.

Ellul, Jacques. *Money and Power.* Downers Grove: Inter-Varsity Press, 1984.

"Executive Pay Too High, Workers Say." *National Post*, 27 June, 2007, WK 7.

Flow, Don. "A Business Owner's Mission." In *Faith Goes to Work*, 67-79. Edited by Robert J. Banks. New York: The Alban Institute, 1993.

Forell, George W., Lazareth, William H., eds. *Work As Praise.* Philadelphia: Fortress Press, 1979.

Green, Thomas H. *Darkness in the Marketplace: The Christian at Prayer in the World.* Notre Dame, IN: Ave Maria Press, 1981.

Grisez, Germain. *Personal Vocation.* Huntington: Our Sunday Visitor Publishing, 2003.

Grootenboer, Ed. *About Work and Unions*. London, ON: Christian Labour Association of Canada, 1984.

Grueneberg, Mary Ellen. Leduc Alliance Church, Leduc, Alberta, Canada, 2005.

Hahn, H. C. "ergadzomai." In *The New International Dictionary of New Testament Theology*. Vol III, 1147-1152. Edited by Colin Brown. Grand Rapids: Zondervan, 1975.

Hardy, Lee. *The Fabric of This World*. Grand Rapids: Eerdmans, 1990.

Harm, F. R. "Sabbatarianism." In *Evangelical Dictionary of Theology*, Edited by Walter A. Elwell. 963-964. Grand Rapids: Baker, 1984.

Haughey, John C. *Converting 9 to 5*. New York: Crossroads, 1989.

________., ed. *Revisiting the Idea of Vocation*. Washington: The Catholic University of America Press, 2004.

Hauwerwas, Stanley. "Work as Co-Creation: A Critique of a Remarkably Bad Idea," 42-58. In *Co-Creation and Capitalism*. Edited by John W. Houck and Oliver F. Williams. Lanham: University Press of America, 1983.

Henry, Carl. *Aspects of Christian Social Ethics*. Grand Rapids: Eerdmans, 1964.

Holland, Joe. *Creative Communion—Towards a Spirituality of Work*. New York: Paulist Press, 1989.

Humphreys, Kent. *Lasting Investments*. Colorado Springs: Navpress, 2004.

Jacobs, and Krienke, H. "protithami." In *The New International Dictionary of New Testament Theology*, vol. 1, p 697-701. Edited by Colin Brown.

Jacobsen, Steve, *Hearts to God, Hands to Work*. New York: The Alban Institute, 1997.

Kaiser, Edwin G. *Theology of Work*. Westminster, Maryland: The Newman Press, 1966.

Kass, Leon. *The Hungry Soul: Eating and the Perfecting of Our Nature*. Chicago: University of Chicago Press, 1999. Quoted in Paul Stevens, *Down to Earth Spirituality*, 36. Downers Grove: Intervarsity Press, 2003.

Kouzes, James M and Posner, Barry Z. *The Leadership Challenge*. 3rd ed. San Francisco: Jossey-Bass, 2002.

Lowery, D.K. "Lord's Day." In *Evangelical Dictionary of Theology*, 648-650. Edited by Walter A. Elwell. Grand Rapids: Baker, 1984.

MacLeod, George F. *Only One Way Left*. Glasgow: The Iona Community, n.d.

Marshall, Paul. "Vocation, Work, and Jobs." In *Labour of Love*. Josina Van Nuis Zylstra, 1-19. Toronto: Wedge Publishing, 1980.

McCann, Dennis. "Apology for the Hireling." *Christian Century*, May 17/95, 542-545.

McCurley, Foster R. and Reumann, John H. "Work in the Providence of God." In *Work as Praise*, 26-42. Edited by George W. Forell and William H. Lazareth. Philadelphia: Fortress Press, 1979.

Mestre, Michel and Sutherland, John R. "The Difference a Worldview Makes." In *Us and Them*, 45-60. Edited by John R. Sutherland. Mississauga: Work Research Foundation, 1999.

Moore, Thomas. *A Life At Work*. New York: Broadway Books, 2008.

Mouw, Richard. *Called to Holy Worldliness*. Philadelphia: Fortress Press, 1980.

Nijkamp, Peter. "Socioethical Aspects of Labour." In *Labour of Love*, 48-66. Edited by Josina Van Nuis Zylstra. Toronto: Wedge Publishing, 1980.

Novak, Michael "Creation Theology." In *Co-Creation and Capitalism*, 17-41. Edited by John W. Houck and Oliver F. Williams. Lanham: University Press of America, 1983.

Ogilvie, Lloyd J., gen. ed. *The Communicator's Commentary, Old Testament*, 21 vols. Waco: Word, 1987. Vol. 2: *Exodus* by Maxie D. Dunnam.

Oswalt, John N. "beraka." In *Theological Wordbook of the Old Testament*, Vol. 1, 132-133. Edited by R. Laird Harris, Gleason L. Archer, Jr., Bruce K. Waltke. Chicago: Moody, 1980.

_______. "kabash." In *Theological Wordbook of the Old Testament*. Vol. 1, 430. Edited by R. Laird Harris, Gleason L. Archer, Jr., Bruce K. Waltke. Chicago: Moody, 1980.

Palmer, Parker. *Let Your Life Speak: Listening for the Voice of Vocation*. San Francisco: Jossey-Bass, 2000.

Perkins, William. "A Treatise of the Vocations." In Callings, 262-273. Edited by William C. Placher. Grand Rapids: Eerdmans, 2005.

Pope Jean Paul II. *Laborem Exercens*. Washington: Office of Publishing and Promotion Services, United States Catholic Conference, 1981.

_______, *Laborem Exercens*. Quoted in Stanley Hauerwas, "Work as Co-Creation: A Critique of a Remarkably Bad Idea," 42-58. In *Co-Creation and Capitalism*. Edited by John W. Houck and Oliver F. Williams. Lanham: University Press of America, 1983.

Preece, Gordon. "Work." In *The Marketplace Ministry Handbook*, 303-310. Edited by Paul Stevens and Robert Banks. Vancouver: Regent College Publishing, 2005.

Rienecker, Fritz. *A Linguistic Key to the Greek New Testament.* Translated by Cleon L. Rogers, Jr. Grand Rapids: Zondervan, 1982.

Richardson, Alan, *The Biblical Doctrine of Work.* Liverpool and London: Charles Birchall & Sons Ltd., 1963.

Robertson, H. M. *Aspects of the Rise of Economic Individualism.* New York: Kelly and Millman, 1959. Quoted in Ryken, *Work and Leisure in Christian Perspective,* 134. Portland: Multnomah, 1987.

Robinson, Haddon. "What Authority Do We Have Anymore?" In *Making a Difference in Preaching,* 29-39. Edited by Scott M. Gibson. Grand Rapids: Baker, 1999.

Ryan, Robin. *What to Do with the Rest of Your Life.* New York: Simon and Schuster, 2002.

Ryken, Leland. *Work and Leisure in Christian Perspective.* Portland: Multnomah, 1987.

Sample, Tex. *Blue-Collar Ministry.* Valley Forge: Judson Press, 1984.

Sayers, Dorothy. *Creed or Chaos.* London: Methuen & Co., 1942.

________. *Why Work*? London: Methuen & Co., 1942. Quoted in Leland Ryken, *Work and Leisure in Christian Perspective,* 174. Portland: Multnomah, 1987.

Sherman, Doug. *Keeping Your Head Up When Your Job's Got You Down.* Brentwood, TN: Wolgemuth & Hyatt, 1991.

Sherman, Doug and Hendricks, William. *Your Work Matters to God.* Colorado Springs: NavPress, 1987.

Shoemaker, Sam et al. *Steps to a New Beginning.* Nashville: Thomas Nelson, 1993.

Shostak, Arthur B. *Blue-collar Life*. New York: Random House, 1969.

Shriver, Donald W. "Vocation and Work in an Era of Downsizing." In *Christian Century*, May 17/95, 538-540.

Shriver, Peggy. "Hard Work." In *Christian Century*, May 17/95, 540-542.

Sider, Ronald J. *One-Sided Christianity*. Grand Rapids: Zondervan, 1993.

Smith-Moran, Barbara. *Soul at Work*. Winona: Saint Mary's Press, 1997.

Statistics Canada. Labour Force Historical Review 2008 (Table Cd1 Ti0an). Ottawa. Statistics Canada, 2009 (Cat. No. 71F0004XCB).

Stevens, Paul. *Doing God's Business*. Grand Rapids: Eerdmans, 2006.

________. *The Other Six Days: Vocation, Work and Ministry in Biblical Perspective*. Grand Rapids: Eerdmans and Vancouver: Regent Publishing, 1999.

________. "Calling/Vocation." In *The Marketplace Ministry Handbook*, 33-40. Edited by Paul Stevens and Robert Banks. Vancouver: Regent College Publishing, 2005.

Stott, John. "Reclaiming the Biblical Doctrine of Work." *Christianity Today*, May 4, 1979. Quoted in Leland Ryken, *Work and Leisure in Christian Perspective*, 164. Portland: Multnomah, 1987.

Sutherland, John. "Who Needs Unions? We Do!" In *The Marketplace*, September/October, 1995, 20.

________. "A Union Run by Christians." In *The Marketplace*, July/August, 2000, 11.

Terkel, Studs. *Working: People Talk About What They Do All Day and How They Feel About What They Do.* New York: Pantheon Books, 1972.

Terzick, Peter. "I am a Building Tradesman," In *Of Human Hands,* 47-48. Edited by Gregory F. Augustine Pierce. Minneapolis: Augsburg, 1991.

The Second Vatican Ecumenical Council, Pastoral Constitution on the Church in the Modern World, "Gaudium et Spes," 39:AAs 58, 1966. Quoted in Stanley Hauerwas, "Work as Co-creation: A Critique of a Remarkably Bad Idea," 42-58. In *Co-Creation and Capitalism*. Edited by John W. Houck and Oliver F. Williams. Lanham: University Press of America, 1983.

Volf, Miroslav. *Work in the Spirit.* New York: Oxford University Press, 1991.

Weinberg, Steven. *The First Three Minutes.* New York: Basic Books, 1998. Quoted in Barbara Smith-Moran, *Soul at Work,* 94. Winona: Saint Mary's Press, 1997.

"We're Just a Bunch of Whiners." *National Post,* 27 June, 2007, WK4.

Wilton, Suzanne. "With God on Their Side." In *Alberta Venture Magazine,* May, 2006, 59-64.

Wingren, Gustaf. *The Christian's Calling: Luther on Vocation.* Translated by C. C. Rasmussen. Edinburgh: Oliver and Boyd, 1957.

"Women Spend Twice as Much Time as Men on Chores." *The Daily Telegraph Online,* 6 October, 2009.

Young, E. J. and Bruce, F. F. "Sabbath." In *New Bible Dictionary.* 1042-1043. Edited by J. D. Douglas. Leicester: Inter-Varsity, 1962.

www.ingramcontent.com/pod-product-compliance
Ingram Content Group UK Ltd.
Pitfield, Milton Keynes, MK11 3LW, UK
UKHW041944190726
13854UKWH00004B/1785

9 781449 724733